ABOUT THE AUTHORS

Tim Callan is a Senior Research Officer at The Economic and Social Research Institute.

Brian Nolan is a Research Professor at The Economic and Social Research Institute.

Brendan J. Whelan is Director of The Economic and Social Research Institute.

Christopher T. Whelan is a Research Professor at The Economic and Social Research Institute.

James Williams is a Senior Research Officer and Head of the Survey Unit at The Economic and Social Research Institute.

POVERTY IN THE 1990s

EVIDENCE FROM THE 1994
LIVING IN IRELAND SURVEY

Tim Callan
Brian Nolan
Brendan J. Whelan
Christopher T. Whelan
James Williams

Oak Tree Press
Dublin

Oak Tree Press
Merrion Building
Lower Merrion Street
Dublin 2, Ireland

A catalogue record of this book is
available from the British Library.

_..l_

ISBN 1-86076-037-6

This study forms part of The Economic and Social Research Institute's
General Research Series, in which it is Paper No. 170. It has been
subject to the normal internal and external refereeing procedures
employed for that series and accepted for publication by the Institute,
which does not itself take institutional policy decisions.

It also forms part of the Combat Poverty Agency's Research Series, in
which it is No. 23. The view expressed in this report are the authors'
own and not necessarily those of the Combat Poverty Agency.

Printed in Ireland by Colour Books Ltd.

CONTENTS

ACKNOWLEDGEMENTS

This study arises from a major research programme being carried out at The Economic and Social Research Institute and sponsored by the Department of Social Welfare and the Combat Poverty Agency. It relies on a new and unique data source, the 1994 Living in Ireland Survey, which constitutes the Irish element of the European Community Household Panel initiated by Eurostat, the Statistical Office of the European Communities. It will be followed in the course of that programme by further studies exploiting the potential of this database for comparative and dynamic analysis of poverty and tax and social welfare policy.

In carrying out this study we owe an enormous debt to the members of the research programme's Steering Committee. Anne Vaughan, Brian O'Raghallaigh and Ann-Marie O'Connor of the Department of Social Welfare and Helen Johnston and Sarah Craig of the Combat Poverty Agency have been deeply involved throughout, from the design of the survey all the way through to providing detailed and insightful comments on various drafts. We wish to acknowledge the importance of their contribution.

We also gratefully acknowledge the comments and suggestions of the two internal ESRI referees, Alan Barrett and Dorothy Watson, as well as those of the anonymous external referee. The staff of the ESRI Survey Unit, the interviewers, and the survey respondents are all to be thanked for their efforts, without which this study would not have been possible. We also wish to thank Pat Hopkins, Maura Rohan, Mary McElhone and Deirdre Whitaker for their usual unfailing assistance.

We accept full responsibility for the content and for any errors or omissions.

LIST OF TABLES

LIST OF FIGURES

GENERAL SUMMARY

This study makes use of data from a new source, the 1994 Living in Ireland Survey, to analyse the extent and nature of poverty in Ireland and how they have been changing over time. An extensive body of research on poverty and related issues has been produced using the household survey carried out in 1987 by the ESRI. The 1994 survey, the Irish element of a new European Community Household Panel, offers an invaluable opportunity to update the picture presented by that research and deepen our understanding of poverty and anti-poverty policy. This initial study, carried out as part of a programme of research being sponsored by the Department of Social Welfare and the Combat Poverty Agency, analyses the extent of poverty and the risk and incidence of poverty for different types of households, and how this has been changing over time.

MEASURING POVERTY OVER TIME

In examining how poverty has changed between 1987 and 1994, the key methodological issue is how the standards applied to distinguish between the poor and the non-poor should be updated over time, in particular whether they should be adjusted to take only price changes into account or whether they should move in line with average incomes. The study first addresses this issue at the conceptual level, reviewing the variety of approaches which have been adopted to measuring poverty over time in academic studies and in current official practice in the UK, the USA, and the European Union. Against this background, the view taken in this study is that over any significant period, poverty thresholds indexed only to prices will lose touch with everyday spending patterns and expectations. Over a relatively short period, however, the way real as well as relative incomes evolve will affect perceptions of income adequacy. While relying primarily on purely relative income lines, we therefore also look at the way numbers under thresholds held constant in real terms since 1987 have changed. As in our research with 1987 data, we also combine relative income lines with non-monetary deprivation indicators in order to hone in on those experiencing generalised deprivation due to lack of resources.

THE DATA

Since this is the first time the data from the 1994 Living in Ireland Survey have been used in this context, a detailed description of the survey itself is provided. This covers the way the survey was designed and carried out, the data gathered, the post-sampling processing of the data, the reweighting procedures adopted, and validation of the representativeness and reliability of the data. The survey appears to represent satisfactorily important features of the population, including the age and sex distribution, numbers at work and unemployed, and numbers in receipt of the major social welfare schemes.

CHANGES IN INCOME POVERTY, 1987–1994

A central element of the study is the application of relative income poverty lines to the 1994 data on household incomes, to see how the numbers below these lines have changed since 1987. Relative income lines represent a proportion of average income, and thus move up over time in line with that average. Between 1987 and 1994, average household income (adjusted to take differences in household size and composition into account) rose by about 50 per cent. With consumer prices rising by about 21 per cent over the same period, this represents a substantial increase in real terms. The poverty line set at half average income in 1994 is about £63.00 per week for a single person. Alternative lines set at 40 per cent and 60 per cent of the average are about £50.00 and £75.00 respectively.

Compared with 1987, the proportion of persons below the 50 per cent and even more so the 60 per cent line is found to have increased by 1994, though the percentage below the 40 per cent relative line fell or was stable. With the highest, 60 per cent, line the poverty rate is 3-4 percentage points higher in 1994 than in 1987.

Simply counting the number of persons below an income threshold takes no account of how far below it they fall. We therefore also present alternative aggregate poverty measures which take into account the depth of poverty shortfalls as well as numbers below the relative income lines. These measures show a consistent fall in aggregate poverty between 1987 and 1994. Indeed, these summary measures are found to be lower in 1994 than they had been back in 1973, when the simple head-count of persons below the income lines was significantly lower. The depth of income shortfalls for those below the income lines has fallen over time, and particularly since 1987.

As well as purely relative income lines, the numbers under income thresholds held constant in real terms since 1987 are also examined. The growth in average real incomes which took place over the period is seen to have benefited those on low incomes, with a substantial decline in the numbers below thresholds held constant from 1987. For example, about 20 per cent of persons were below half average income in 1987; by 1994 only about 8 per cent were below that line uprated by the increase in prices over the period.

RISK AND INCIDENCE OF INCOME POVERTY

Using the relative income lines, the study analyses poverty risk and incidence in 1994 by household composition and by labour force status, and compares the results with 1987. This comparison with 1987 shows a good deal of continuity, as would be expected, but also some important differences. The most striking decline in poverty risk is for farm households. On the other hand, the risk of being below the 50 or 60 per cent relative lines has increased for single-adult households, the elderly, female-headed households and households headed by someone "in home duties" — working full-time in the home — with a good deal of overlap between these groups. With the 50 per cent relative income line, about one-third of poor households in 1994 are headed by an unemployed person, with the second-largest group being those headed by someone in home duties. Children face a higher risk of being below the income lines than adults, and households with four or more children are at particularly high risk, as are lone parent households.

LOW INCOME AND DEPRIVATION

In addition to analysing household incomes, non-monetary indicators of deprivation are used to identify those experiencing generalised deprivation or exclusion due to lack of resources — a definition of poverty in common use in developed countries, though not often implemented. Deprivation indicators on which information was obtained in the 1994 survey are mostly the same as those included in the 1987 survey and used in our previous research. Compared with the 1987 survey, the percentage of households doing without the various items or activities has generally fallen by 1994. Focusing on a sub-set of items representing basic deprivation, there has been a small reduction between 1987 and 1994 in the percentage of households both below the relative income poverty lines and experiencing basic deprivation. For example, in 1987, 16 per cent of households were below the 60 per cent income line and experiencing enforced absence of at least one basic item, while in 1994 the corresponding figure was 15 per cent

Distinguishing households as poor using both income and basic deprivation once again produces a poverty profile that differs significantly from simply applying income lines, with fewer households headed by a farmer or other self-employed among the poor and more headed by someone who is retired or in home duties. Households with an unemployed head continue to be the most substantial group among the poor using a combination of income and deprivation information.

UNDERSTANDING THE CHANGES IN INCOME POVERTY

The falling risk of poverty for farm households is directly attributable to the fact that the year covered by the 1987 survey was an unusually bad one for income from agriculture, and farm incomes have increased substantially since then. This will also have had a particularly pronounced impact on the summary poverty measures taking the extent to which people fall below the income lines into account, since these will be significantly affected by the numbers reporting zero or very low incomes.

The evolution of social welfare rates for different categories of recipient *vis-à-vis* mean income for all households plays a crucial role in explaining other aspects of the results. As recommended by the Commission on Social Welfare, priority was given from 1987 to raising what were then the lowest social welfare rates, for Unemployment Assistance and Supplementary Welfare Allowance. Rates for these schemes thus increased a good deal more rapidly than mean incomes between 1987 and 1994. However, the scale of increase sufficed to bring recipients of those schemes much closer to, but not quite up to, the 50 per cent relative income line by

1994. At the same time support rates for other groups, notably the elderly and widows, rose by a good deal less than mean incomes. As a result, by 1994 many of those relying on old age or widow's pensions were on incomes at or about the 50 per cent line and below the 60 per cent one, whereas in 1987 they had been comfortably above half average income.

A major plank of social welfare strategy over the period — giving priority to the lowest rates — brought recipients a good deal closer to the line but had limited impact on reducing the numbers falling below half average income, while the associated relative decline in the support provided to other groups increased their vulnerability. This helps to explain the fact that poverty measures taking the extent to which people fall below the 50 and 60 per cent relative income lines were stable or fell while the headcount of numbers below those lines rose. This brings out the importance of using those more complex summary measures as complements to simply "counting the poor". The substantial rise in social welfare support rates in real terms, as well as the rapid rise in farm incomes and the fall in the level of unemployment between 1987 and 1994, are the major factors explaining the sharp fall in numbers below income lines uprated for price increases only. They also underlie the much smaller decline in numbers below relative income lines and experiencing basic deprivation.

FUTURE RESEARCH USING THE NEW SURVEY DATA

Building on this initial study, priorities for further research on poverty using the 1994 data will be to explore a detailed analysis of the variation in poverty risk and incidence across a broader range of individual and household characteristics than are covered here. The relationship between income and deprivation indicators will also be examined in greater depth. The impact of changes in the tax and social welfare systems between 1987 and 1994 will be examined, to point up the impact of policy versus exogenous factors on the extent and composition of poverty in Ireland over that period. The fact that the same set of households have been reinterviewed in 1995 and 1996, as part of the European Community Household Panel, will open up new possibilities for exploring short-term income and poverty dynamics. Finally, since these Irish surveys form part of a harmonised EU-wide panel there will be enormous potential to learn from cross-country comparisons on poverty rates and incidence, the effectiveness of different policy regimes, and income and labour force dynamics. This body of research, like the present study, will be an important input into policy formation, in particular the development and monitoring of the National Anti-Poverty Strategy.

December 1996

Chapter 1

INTRODUCTION

This study presents the first results from the 1994 Living in Ireland Survey on the extent and nature of poverty in Ireland in 1994 and how this has changed since 1987. Thanks to the extensive body of research made possible by the Survey of Income Distribution, Poverty and Use of State Services carried out by the ESRI in 1987 and supported by the Department of Social Welfare, the Combat Poverty Agency and the European Commission, we know a great deal about the extent of low income and deprivation and the types of household at risk of poverty in the mid- to late-1980s. (For an overview of this research, see Nolan and Callan, 1994.) The opportunity has now arisen to update and extend this research on the basis of the 1994 Living in Ireland Survey.

This new survey is the Irish element of a major initiative entitled the European Community Household Panel (ECHP) which is being funded and co-ordinated by the European Statistical Office, Eurostat. The aim of this ambitious study, which is currently under way on a collaborative basis in all the Member States of the European Union, is to follow a large random sample of households through time to examine the nature and causes of changes in income, labour market experiences and many other aspects of people's lives. The data analysed in this report comprise the first wave of the ECHP in Ireland. Additional support for this wave was provided by the Department of Social Welfare and the Combat Poverty Agency in order (a) to supplement the basic ECHP questionnaire by the addition of a number of questions which were of particular importance in the Irish context, and (b) to sponsor an agreed programme of research. In this first study, we focus on the question of primary interest both to policy-makers and more broadly: how has the extent and composition of poverty in Ireland changed since 1987?

The central methodological issue to be faced in answering this question is how best to measures changes in poverty over time. Chapter 2 addresses this issue at the conceptual level, reviewing the variety of approaches which have been adopted to measuring poverty over time in academic studies and in current official practice in the UK, the USA, and the European Union. The approaches to be adopted in this study are then sketched out against that background.

Chapter 3 provides a description of the 1994 Living in Ireland Survey and the data it produces, on which the study relies. This covers the way the survey itself was designed and carried out, the data gathered, the post-sampling processing of the data, the reweighting procedures to be adopted, and validation of the representativeness and reliability of the data.

Chapter 4 applies income poverty lines to the 1994 data on household incomes. The results provide a picture of the overall pattern in terms of numbers below a range of income poverty lines in 1994. The way the numbers below relative income lines have evolved since 1987 is analysed, and alternative aggregate poverty measures are presented which take into account the depth of poverty shortfalls as well as numbers below the income lines. A longer-term comparison is also made with 1980 and 1973 using the Household Budget Surveys for those years. As well as purely relative lines, the numbers under income thresholds held constant in real terms since 1987 are also examined.

Chapter 5 uses relative income poverty lines to analyse poverty risk and incidence by household composition and by labour force status of the household head. The pattern found is then compared with the corresponding results for 1987, and the main similarities and differences are brought out.

Chapter 6 focuses on non-monetary deprivation indicators, which our work with the 1987 survey data has shown can, in combination with information on incomes, provide a more reliable way than income lines alone of identifying those experiencing generalised deprivation due to lack of resources. The deprivation indicators employed in the 1994 survey are first described, and the extent to which the households in the sample lack the items or activities in question is then discussed and compared with 1987. The way in which the deprivation indicators relate to one another is then analysed. Three separate summary indices are constructed, representing what we have termed in previous work the basic, housing and secondary dimensions, and their relationships with household income analysed. Those households falling below relative income lines and experiencing basic deprivation are then identified and their characteristics in terms of labour force status compared with those simply below the income lines. The numbers and types of household distinguished in this manner are compared with 1987.

Finally, Chapter 7 briefly brings together the key findings and sets out some of the priorities for further research on poverty using the 1994 data.

Chapter 2

THE MEASUREMENT OF POVERTY OVER TIME

2.1 INTRODUCTION

This study is concerned with measuring the extent and nature of poverty in Ireland in 1994 and how this has changed since 1987. Thanks to the extensive body of research made possible by the 1987 Survey of Income Distribution, Poverty and Use of State Services, we know a great deal about the extent of low income and deprivation and the types of household at risk of poverty in that year. In presenting in this study the first results from the 1994 Living in Ireland Survey, we will be focusing on the question of primary interest both to policy-makers and more broadly: how has the extent and composition of poverty changed since 1987? The central methodological issue to be faced in answering this question is how to choose a poverty standard for application in 1994 which best measures changes over time.

In this chapter we address this issue at the conceptual level, reviewing the variety of approaches which have been adopted to measuring poverty over time in academic studies and official practice. This involves first reviewing briefly the way poverty has generally been conceptualised in developed countries, focusing on the core question in looking at changes over time, which is the extent to which poverty is conceived in relative versus absolute terms. The different approaches to deriving and applying a poverty standard (which we have discussed at length in previous work) are then briefly examined to bring out the implications for the way the poverty standard is adjusted over time. We then look at current official practice in the UK, the USA, and the European Union, which provide particularly interesting and relevant points of reference. Finally, we set out in broad terms the approaches which will be adopted in this study.

2.2 CONCEPTS AND MEASURES

In everyday use, poverty in developed countries is often seen as an inability to attain a "decent" or "adequate" living standard. What is considered adequate, what are generally perceived as "needs", will change over time and differ across societies: poverty is in that sense relative. This is not a new definition, since poverty has always been defined in relation to the standards with which people in a particular time and place are familiar. In this study, once again, we take as a starting-point Townsend's definition of poverty:

> Individuals, families and groups in the population can be said to be in poverty when they lack the resources to obtain the type of diet, participate in the activities and have the living conditions and amenities which are customary, or at least widely encouraged, or approved, in the societies to which they belong. Their resources are so seriously below those commanded by the average individual or family that they are, in effect, excluded from ordinary living patterns, customs and activities (1979, p. 31).

This emphasis on participation versus exclusion serves to make explicit the relative nature of the concept and has been widely adopted in recent discourse on poverty in developed countries.

There are some dissenting voices who see poverty as primarily an absolute notion, but the dominant view is that expressed by Piachaud: "Close to subsistence level there is indeed some absolute minimum necessary for survival but apart from this, any poverty standard must reflect prevailing social standards: it must be a relative standard" (1987, p. 148). In practice, as we discuss in more detail below, standards presented as aiming to measure "absolute" poverty in developed countries do not apply a timeless, fixed poverty line based on an unchanging set of minimum needs. In fact, they are heavily influenced by prevailing conditions and expenditure patterns. Their true distinguishing feature is the way the poverty standard is adjusted over time, being uprated simply in line with prices and taking no account of changes in average income or expenditure patterns. The concept of poverty which we adopt in this as in previous studies is Townsend's one of exclusion resulting from lack of resources. This is inherently and explicitly a relative conception. We believe there is also a value in assessing change against a standard held fixed in real terms — as Lampman (1971) put it, in fighting a "War on Poverty" one may want to monitor how well one is doing in meeting a fixed target rather than redefining the target as income changes. In this study we look not only at relative poverty standards but also at changes *vis-à-vis* standards indexed to prices between 1987 and 1994. However, such fixed standards fail to capture what is inherent in the everyday understanding of the notion of poverty, that the standards being applied will be socially determined and will change over time as incomes rise and living patterns change, and we do not therefore regard them as satisfactory measures of poverty.

Measuring poverty involves two distinct elements: deciding on the indicator or yardstick on which to focus in measuring poverty, and deriving a poverty standard applying to that yardstick. Here Sen (1979) has emphasised the importance of the conceptual distinction between what he calls the "direct" approach of identifying the poor in terms of inability to meet minimum consumption levels, and the "income" method of comparing household income with the cost of a minimum consumption basket: the former identifies those whose actual consumption levels across a range of commodities fail to meet minimum accepted levels, while the latter identifies those who do not have the *ability* to attain those levels (within the behavioural constraints on expenditure patterns typical in their community) (see Sen, 1979, pp. 290-1). Atkinson (1987) makes the related distinction between a concern with the attainment of a *minimum standard of living* and with people's rights as citizens to a *minimum level of resources*, the disposal of which is a matter for them; entitlement to a minimum level of resources is seen both as a reward for citizenship and as a prerequisite for participation in society. In the same vein Ringen makes a distinction between poverty as deprivation — people are poor if their standard of consumption is seriously below what is considered decent in their society — and poverty as lack of resources — people are poor if they do not have the resources deemed necessary to achieve a certain minimum level of consumption (1988, p. 353-4).

These distinctions are not as straightforward as they might appear, and there is a good deal of confusion in the literature surrounding them. The scope for confusion is partly, but not entirely, attributable to the point stressed by both Atkinson and Ringen, that it is common to define the poverty line in terms of living standards but then use income (or less often expenditure) in assessing whether a household falls below it. The poverty standard itself can be derived in a variety of ways, ranging from the basket

of goods or "budget standard" approach, the food ratio method, social security payment rates, perceptions of minimally adequate income, the average level of income in the society, or observed living
standards at different income levels. Direct non-monetary indicators of deprivation have been used by Townsend (1979) to derive an
income standard and by Mack and Lansley (1985) to directly identify the poor. Ringen has argued for a combination of income and
deprivation information in identifying the poor, to ensure that those
so identified are indeed experiencing exclusion due to lack of resources. In previous work based on the 1987 survey data for Ireland, as well as applying income poverty lines, we have developed
an approach to combining income and deprivation indicators, demonstrating the value of that combination in the analysis of poverty
(Callan, Nolan and Whelan, 1993; Nolan and Whelan, 1996).

The value we see in using both income and indicators of deprivation, rather than income alone, is that one can identify more
accurately those excluded from the ordinary life of society due to
lack of resources. It does not represent a shift from measuring
poverty to measuring "social exclusion", the term which has recently replaced poverty in official EU usage, and is now quite
commonly used together with or instead of poverty in academic
and official discourse.[1] Social exclusion has remained a rather ill-
defined and amorphous concept. Some regard it as a conceptual
advance on poverty because it is dynamic rather than static,
about processes rather than situations, and is about the range of
dimensions across which exclusion can be experienced rather
than "only" about financial resources. As discussed at length in
Nolan and Whelan (1996), this contrast is to a considerable extent
based on a caricature of the concept of poverty, which can itself be
viewed and measured in a way which highlights dynamics, processes and multidimensionality. We see two major disadvantages
with a wholesale switch from a focus on poverty to social exclusion. The first is that this would replace a term which has deep
resonance at popular level with one which does not. The second is
that social exclusion is insufficiently well-defined at this point,
and seeking to implement it empirically could obscure rather
than highlight the central processes at work. We continue to con-

---

[1] For example, in the course of developing the National Anti-Poverty Strategy
an Inter-departmental Policy Committee has recently produced a Consul-
tative Overview Statement on "Poverty, Social Exclusion and Inequality in
Ireland" (1995).

centrate here on the measurement of poverty and the identification of the factors at work in producing it. In the next section we discuss alternative approaches to measuring poverty over time.

2.3 APPROACHES TO MEASURING POVERTY OVER TIME

The Budget Standard Approach

The budget standard method, as employed by Rowntree in his pioneering British studies and in the construction of the US official poverty line (which is discussed in more detail below), is based initially on the specification and costing of a nutritionally adequate diet. Non-food expenditures can then be taken into account either by specifying and costing requirements for each commodity or group of commodities — such as clothing, housing, transport — or by simply multiplying the "necessary" food expenditure by a factor, to reflect the relationship between food and non-food expenditure considered to be desirable. This method, on the face of it, has a number of appealing features. First, the required expenditures are apparently being calculated in an objective and scientific manner. Secondly, it allows a line to be specified which can be taken to represent a fixed basket of goods and services, which are believed to represent the bare necessities of life (as Sawhill (1988) puts it in discussing the US line). This can then be indexed to prices, and progress against this fixed poverty line over time can be monitored.

However, the extent and nature of the judgements being made need to be emphasised. Even for food, nutritional studies do not permit a precise estimate of what is "needed".[2] For other expenditures, and to some extent for food as well, "needs" as defined by experts — both the commodities deemed to be necessities and the minimum quantity required — will be based on what are in effect social rather than scientific criteria, and with a significant degree of arbitrariness. In addition, most budget standards have in practice made allowances for items which are not considered necessities, and for the fact that consumers do not actually allocate their expenditure "optimally"; again, the scope for judgement and arbitrariness is wide. As we shall see, judgement and/or arbitrariness

---

[2] As Atkinson (1983) has stressed, there is "rather a broad range where physical efficiency declines with falling intake of calories and proteins" (p. 226).

also characterise other commonly-used approaches to deriving an income poverty line, but with the budget standards method there is greater danger that this may not be apparent.

The budget standard poverty lines cannot therefore be seen as representing requirements which are in any sense "absolute" or needed for subsistence: the terminology employed can give the misleading impression that an immutable set of "needs" is being measured. They can serve as the basis for a line which is then held fixed over time in real terms, as in the US official poverty line discussed below, but there is no reason why such a fixed standard has to be based initially on the budget standard method. The debate about "absolute" versus "relative" poverty, which is central to the measurement of changes in poverty over time, hinges not on whether poverty should be assessed on the basis of a set of requirements absolutely necessary for subsistence, but rather whether the poverty line should be held fixed in real terms over time or rise as the general standard of living in the society rises. As already noted, in our view assessing change against a standard fixed in real terms provides important information, particularly over a short period, but it can quite quickly lose touch with what people in the society actually regard as poverty.

Costing a specified consumption basket does have a role to play in assessing the adequacy of social security support, while explicitly acknowledging that the "needs" involved are socially defined and that there is a substantial element of judgement and arbitrariness involved. For example, Piachaud's (1979) analysis of the cost of a specified consumption bundle for children in Britain showed that support rates for teenagers were less generous than those for younger children relative to their "needs", and Bradshaw and Morgan's (1987) costing of a basket of goods illustrated that those on social security could afford only "an extremely restricted and dull lifestyle" (p. 14), with food consumption deficient in nutrition. Following the same approach, the Irish study of *The Cost of a Child* by Carney et al. (1994) showed that in 1992 child income support levels for social welfare recipients (taking both Child Dependant Additions and Child Benefit into account) were well below the cost of what the authors considered a basic minimum consumption basket for older children. The main potential of the budget standards approach is thus, in our view, in demonstrating in concrete terms the standard of living which can actually be attained at specific income levels, in the light of observed spending patterns.

The Food-Ratio Method

The food-ratio method has the appeal of simplicity, in terms of its conceptual basis. It is based on the observation (first credited to Engel in 1895) that the proportion of income spent on necessities tends to fall as incomes rise. A threshold distinguishing the poor from the non-poor can be framed either in terms of the income level at which a specified proportion spent on necessities is just reached on average, or in terms of the target proportion itself. The former approach is employed by Statistics Canada to produce "low-income cut-offs": the Engel Curve relationship (between the proportion spent on necessities and income, controlling for other relevant variables such as family size and location) is used to produce an income line at which a specified proportion of spending goes on necessities on average. In constructing the Low Income Cut-offs (LICOs) — which Statistics Canada repeatedly insists are not official poverty lines — the cut-off proportion is simply the overall average percentage of household expenditures going on necessities plus an arbitrary figure. The definition of "necessities" raises many issues, since simply taking all expenditure on food, clothing and housing includes luxury items such as caviar and fur coats, and excludes other types of expenditures which might be considered necessities. The proportion of expenditure going on necessities varies widely at any given income level — Engel's Law holds only approximately — so a significant number of those below the derived income threshold will not be spending more than the cut-off proportion on necessities, while some of those above the line will be doing so. The critical question is how the poverty lines are to be changed over time: are they to be indexed to consumer prices, or are they also to be revised as consumer expenditure patterns change, and if so how often? In the Canadian case, because the Family Expenditure Survey from which the LICOs were derived were carried out only every four years, the LICOs were uprated in line with consumer prices in between surveys and then re-estimated every four years. The uneven pattern of "fits and starts" which this produced has been acknowledged officially as a fundamental concern, and was a major factor behind the setting up of a review of the methodology by Stats Canada in the late 1980s (see Wolfson and Evans, 1989).

This review considered a number of options for the updating of the thresholds over time: "absolute" uprating in line with the CPI, updating to reflect both changes in prices and real living standards via linking to median family income, or adoption of both absolute and relative methods and leaving the choice between them to the user. This, the review points out, would "provide information on both the major perspectives regarding the trend in the incidence of low income" (p. 62). Evans (1991) reports that responses to the review were split on the merits of absolute versus relative updating. Arguing that few users will want to judge the incomes of the 1990s by the standards of the 1970s, he suggests that the benchmark be set as a proportion of median income in each year, but that in addition a series going back a limited period — say five years — be constructed by deflating the benchmark by the CPI only. This would allow users to see changes over that period in the incidence of low incomes on a "CPI-updated" as well as a "relatively-updated" basis. This discussion highlights central choices to which we will be returning repeatedly.

The "Social Security" Poverty Line Approach

The approach adopted by Abel-Smith and Townsend (1965) in their pioneering work on poverty in post-war Britain, and by many academic and official studies since then, was to take as a benchmark the rates of income support offered by the social security system's safety net. At its most basic level, this may rest simply on the inference that the State must expect recipients to be able to subsist on this income level. More generally, the assumption can be that these rates represent a consensus on the minimum level of income acceptable in the society, or an official expert view on that minimum.[3] However, while the levels of support may initially have borne some relation to the costs of what were thought to be subsistence standards of diet, clothing, etc., both these levels and their adjustment over time are the product of a complex political process, influenced by many other factors.[4]

The "subsistence" concept involved is clearly relative, influenced by changing standards of living in society generally. Levels

---

[3] In Britain the rates of social security support recommended in the Beveridge report (1942) were in fact influenced by the budget-standard results produced by Rowntree.

[4] The Commission on Social Welfare (1986), in assessing Irish social security rates, was unable to discover an explicit basis for the rates initially set. The range of methods then employed by the Commission to estimate what would constitute "adequate" rates is reviewed in Callan, Nolan and Whelan (1996).

of support provided by the State may rise in line with, or more or less rapidly than, average income in the society, depending on a wide range of influences including the state of the economy, the demands on the social security system, and a variety of socio-political factors. It is, therefore, difficult to accept the status which either the "consensus" or the "expert" interpretation would accord these levels of support as "poverty lines".

The use of social security rates as poverty lines gives rise to obvious anomalies, particularly in measuring changes in poverty over time: although raising the minimum level of social security payments tends to raise the incomes of the poorest groups in society, it will tend to lead to a rise in measured poverty on this definition. Thus, over time such a measure will reflect the combination of changes in the underlying extent of poverty and in the generosity of the social security system's safety net. The application of a "social safety net" line does have the essential function of allowing those who are falling below the social security safety net to be identified and the reasons why explored, so the performance of the social security system in meeting its own minimum income objective can be assessed, but this must be distinguished from the measurement of trends in poverty. In that broader context, the social security system cannot be simply measured against its own standards: an independent standard is required.

Consensual Income Poverty Lines

If the poverty line is to reflect prevailing social standards, one approach is to try to measure views in the population about minimum income needs and derive a line from these responses. Such consensual income poverty lines have been developed primarily in The Netherlands and the US. Theoretical underpinnings have been provided primarily by researchers at Leyden and Tilburg, who have explored the way in which poverty lines may be based on respondents' evaluations of different income levels, and the relationship between these subjective evaluations and welfare. A number of variants of the basic approach have been applied, with varying degrees of sophistication (see Bradbury, 1989). Respondents may be asked:

1. How they would rate particular income levels for a list of hypothetical families of different composition (Dubnoff, 1985), or what income hypothetical families would require to reach different levels of living (Rainwater, 1974)

2. How they feel about their own current income level (Dubnoff, Vaughan and Lancaster, 1981)

3. What income they consider to be the minimum they themselves need to make ends meet (Goedhart et al., 1977)

4. What income levels they would consider, in their own circumstances, to be "very bad", "bad", etc., on a 6-point scale up to "very good" (van Praag et al., 1982).

The most developed forms are the Leyden method employed by van Praag and colleagues (see van Praag et al., 1982; Hagenaars, 1986), and the related Subjective Poverty Line method used by Kapteyn (see Kapteyn, van de Geer and van de Stadt, 1985). The latter is based on responses to question 3 above (the "minimum income question"), which are then related by regression to income and other relevant variables such as household size. For a particular household size, the poverty line is derived as the point where, on average, actual income is equal to the stated minimum income needed. The more complex Leyden method is based on responses to question 4 (the "income evaluation question"), income levels rated on a scale from "very good" to "very bad". Individual "welfare functions of income" are estimated, relating income and welfare evaluations. A critical welfare level must then be chosen (introducing an arbitrary element into the method) and the corresponding level of income derived for each individual. The overall poverty line is then estimated as before, i.e., analysing these derived incomes in the same way as the responses to the minimum income question.

Focusing on changes over time, these approaches have the significant advantage that the poverty standard is updated within the method in line with the responses of those surveyed: no decision has to be taken external to the method itself about an uprating procedure. Some evidence suggests that, when there is real income growth, survey respondents' evaluations of minimum incomes rise by more than the increase in prices alone but less than the full increase in real incomes. One of the difficulties with the consensual approach, however, is that poverty standards produced from a "black box" may not be broadly understood and accepted. Critical assumptions are also involved about the way in which responses to the questions can be interpreted, for example about the relationship between "making ends meet" and what most people would regard as "poverty". It also matters whose views one takes most seriously, since there may in fact be no broad consensus in the sample about the minimum required. Analysis of the way in which perceptions by households of their minimum income needs evolve over time in different circumstances is certainly valuable in itself, particularly perhaps as far as the perceptions of those relying on social welfare are concerned (see Callan, Nolan and Whelan, 1996). The consensual approach was among those applied to Irish data for 1987 in Callan et al. (1989) and will be explored further in future work, but at this point we are not convinced that it provides a satisfactory basis for setting and uprating a poverty standard.

Purely Relative Income Lines

The view that poverty has to be seen in terms of the standard of living of the society in question has led some to frame poverty lines explicitly, and purely, in terms of relative income. Customarily, this involves setting the poverty line at a particular percentage of mean or median income, for example, 50 per cent. The general rationale is that those falling more than a certain "distance" below the average or normal income level in the society are unlikely to be able to participate fully in the life of the community. It should be emphasised that this method is not the same as simply taking the bottom x per cent of the income distribution as "the poor": the number in poverty can then neither rise nor fall, which it clearly can with the poverty line set at, say, 60 per cent of the median. The relative poverty line approach has been adopted in a number of studies by the OECD (1976) and the EC Commission or Eurostat (see, for example, Commission of the European Communities, 1981; O'Higgins and Jenkins, 1990; ISSAS, 1990; Hagenaars et al., 1994). Other cross-country analyses using this approach include Smeeding et al. (1988) and Buhman et al. (1988). This approach also provides the basis for the official British statistics on Households Below Average Income (HBAI), introduced in 1988, replacing a series which had used means-tested income support rates as the benchmark. (Both the Eurostat and British series are described in detail in the next section.)

Under this approach, any improvements in the living standards of low income groups which are shared by the rest of the population are discounted. Likewise, as Sen (1983) points out, a general decline in prosperity, even if it leads to a lot of additional people in misery, will not show up as an increase in poverty if the relative picture has not changed. There is a considerable diversity of views, among those who view poverty primarily in relative terms, about the precise nature of the relativity concerned and therefore the extent to which a purely relative income approach is satisfactory.[5] Most would presumably be much less happy with its application over a period of recession than growth. Even in a steadily growing economy, do socially-perceived "needs" necessarily rise *pari passu* with average incomes? If they are assumed to rise more slowly, then steady income growth from which everyone gained would be guaranteed to eliminate poverty at some future date even if relative positions remained unchanged, with that date depending on the arbitrary choice of base year. Clearly, considerable care needs to be exercised in applying the methodology to specific situations, and it may be more suitable for some than for others. It does have the considerable appeal of simplicity and transparency: it yields results which can be readily understood and serve at least as a starting point for the analysis of poverty, the relative position of low-income groups, and the composition of these groups.

The method does not produce a unique poverty line because the choice of cut-off is arbitrary. Most applications have used 50 per cent of mean or median income, but there is no firm basis for the selection of any particular ratio to serve as *the* poverty line. The application of a range of relative lines has the advantage that it shows the sensitivity of the results to the precise location of the line. This is in the spirit of the approach advocated by Atkinson (1985; 1987) and Foster and Shorrocks (1988a), who argue that the diversity of possible judgements about the specification of the poverty line should be explicitly taken into account in the measurement procedures adopted. Of course, this extends beyond the use of a range of purely relative lines to include lines produced by other approaches: nonetheless, the application of a set of relative lines is a useful first step in making comparisons across countries or over time (see, for example, Buhman et al., 1988; Nolan and Callan, 1989; 1990), and on this basis has been employed extensively in our earlier work on poverty in 1987 and comparing 1987 with 1980 and 1973 using Household Budget Survey data for those years.

---

[5] See, for example, Sen (1983) and Ringen (1988) for an exploration of the issues.

Style of Living and Deprivation

The impetus for focusing directly on patterns of living and deprivation in measuring poverty has come primarily from Townsend's research for Britain (1979). He aimed at analysing styles of living and at developing indicators of objective deprivation, where households lack an amenity or do not participate in activities which a majority of the population have or participate in. Townsend employed a set of twelve items to construct a summary deprivation index, but scores on this index were not used directly to identify the poor. Rather, he tentatively identified an income threshold, representing the point below which deprivation scores "escalated disproportionately". All those below that threshold were then counted as poor, without reference to their deprivation scores. The existence and indeed plausibility of such a threshold continues to be hotly debated, with Piachaud (1987) asserting that it is intrinsically implausible, and that the reality is more accurately described as a continuum from great wealth to chronic poverty. The second major area of criticism relates to the selection of the deprivation indicators and the role of differences in tastes. The particular indicators used were chosen in a rather ad hoc manner, with the degree of judgement required on the part of the researcher widely seen as a problem. At a more general level, Piachaud's influential critique focused also on the substantial variability in the deprivation scores of households at similar income levels. If observed differences in living patterns may be largely attributable to differences in tastes rather than resources, the absence of a particular item or set of items cannot be taken to represent deprivation arising from resource constraints.

Mack and Lansley (1985), by contrast, measured deprivation indicators as socially prescribed necessities and used them directly in identifying the poor. Items were selected for inclusion in their deprivation index on the basis of views in their sample as to what constitutes a necessity. They also asked those who did not have a particular item or engage in a particular activity whether they "would like, but can't afford" that item, "enforced lack" of an item being where the respondent lacked the item *and* said they would like but could not afford it. A deprivation index based on 22 items considered to be necessities by a majority of the sample and also negatively correlated with income was constructed and used to identify the poor. While addressing some of the problems with Townsend's approach, the choice of a particular cut-off point on

Mack and Lansley's deprivation scale is problematic, and the way in which they combine actual lifestyle information, subjective assessments and income to produce a poverty measure is also rather ad hoc. Further, no account is taken of the complex ways in which the relationship between possessions/activities and income or wider resources may vary across different types of item or different household types. Simply adding together items relating to everyday activities with those related to the possession of consumer durables or the quality of housing may also be unsatisfactory as a measure of current living standards/resource constraints.

Subsequent work using non-monetary indicators includes Townsend and Gordon (1989) for Britain, Mayer and Jencks (1988) for the USA and Muffels and Vrien (1991) for The Netherlands. Our own work using 1987 Irish data has developed a methodology to first identify indicators of generalised deprivation, and then apply such indicators in combination with income thresholds in identifying those experiencing deprivation due to lack of resources (Callan, Nolan and Whelan, 1993; Nolan and Whelan, 1996). The key issues this approach identifies and addresses in using indicators of deprivation to measure poverty are:

1. How to select items that are suitable to serve as deprivation indicators

2. How to take into account the role of tastes versus resource constraints as determinants of living patterns

3. How to aggregate deprivation items into a summary index or set of dimensions or otherwise to make use of the information they contain

4. How to select a particular cut-off to distinguish the poor from the non-poor, either on the basis of deprivation scores or using both deprivation and income criteria; and fundamentally, how to elucidate the ways in which the observed deprivation/income pattern comes about.

The way in which our approach deals with these issues is described in Chapter 6 below, where it is applied to the 1994 data for Ireland.

2.4 MEASURING POVERTY OVER TIME IN THE USA, THE UK AND THE EUROPEAN UNION

In order to bring out further the issues which arise in measuring poverty over time, we now describe the way in which this is approached in an official setting in the USA, the UK and the European Union. Of these, only the USA has an official poverty line, but officially-produced statistics in the UK are intended to inform about trends in poverty and living standards, and the Commission of the European Union has sponsored or carried out research on which it has drawn to make statements about the extent of poverty in Member States. It is therefore particularly relevant to see the differences and similarities in the approaches adopted in these three rather different settings.

The USA

As we have seen, the United States is unusual among developed countries in having an official poverty line, and this is based on the budget standard approach. In the mid-1960s, as the War on Poverty commenced, this methodology was used to construct poverty lines for households of given size and composition for the Social Security Administration (see Orshansky, 1965) by taking the Department of Agriculture's so-called "economy food plan" setting out the cost of a nutritionally adequate diet, and multiplying this cost by a factor of three for families of three or more persons. The poverty standards for different household types are uprated from year to year by indexation to the Consumer Price Index. The "headline" official series on the extent of poverty is based on annual household incomes reported in the Current Population Survey (CPS), where persons in families with total money income before tax below the threshold are counted as poor. The main official series produced in this way shows the percentage of persons in poverty in the USA at 22 per cent in 1960, falling to 17 per cent in 1965 and 12 per cent in 1969, remaining at 11-13 per cent during the 1970s, rising in the early 1980s and subsequently fluctuating between about 13-15 per cent.

We have already made the point that poverty lines based on the budget standard approach cannot be said to be "absolute", in the sense of relating to a minimum needed for subsistence or an immutable set of "needs", and the degree of judgement and indeed arbitrariness involved in their construction has also been emphasised. This was pointed out by US critics at an early stage:

Rein (1969), for example, argued that any subsistence-level definition was "arbitrary, circular, and relative". Indeed, Orshansky
herself subsequently wrote that "The link to nutritional economy
and food-income consumption patterns endowed an arbitrary
judgement with a quasi-scientific rationale it otherwise did not
have" (1988, p. 23). The key characteristic is rather that the line is
held fixed over time in real terms. This can lead to conclusions
about trends in poverty over time which differ substantially from
those shown by a purely relative line. For example, when the official poverty standard was introduced in 1965 it came to 46 per
cent of the median (for a family of four), but by 1986 it had fallen
to 32 per cent; while the number below the official line fell over
the period, that below a line maintained at 46 per cent of the median would have risen (see Danziger, Haveman and Plotnick,
1986).

The fact that the poverty standards were originally based on
budget standards and observed consumption behaviour, but are
adjusted over time only in line with prices, also gives rise to internal inconsistency within the logic of the method. It is not only
the general level of prices which changes over time, so do price
relativities, consumption patterns and the goods and services
available for consumption. An approach that relies on price index-
ing alone will fail to take into account these changes, which may
affect the income needed to provide for the "basic necessities"
originally built into the standards. It would be possible to "rebase"
the poverty standards every ten years or so to take such changes
in spending patterns into account, but over any significant period
the whole notion of an unchanging set of necessities itself be-
comes untenable. Ruggles (1990) therefore proposes instead that a
comprehensive budget standard exercise, involving the selection
by "experts" of a minimum basket of goods across the full range,
be done regularly about that often: "if an absolute standard is to
maintain any meaning over several decades it must be updated
periodically" (p. 48). This of course illustrates how misleading the
label "absolute" is, but also highlights the problems with the apparently straightforward and appealing procedure of indexation
of the poverty line to prices over time.

A recent in-depth review of the US official poverty line by a
committee of experts set up by the National Research Council
(Citro and Michael, 1995) emphasised the unsatisfactory nature
of the uprating procedure, pointing out that:

Changes in the standard of living call into question the merits of continuing to use the values of the original thresholds updated only for inflation. Historical evidence suggests that poverty thresholds — including those developed according to "expert" notions of minimum needs — follow trends in overall consumption levels. Because of rising living standards in the United States, most approaches for developing poverty thresholds (including the original one) would produce higher thresholds today than the current ones (p. 2-3).

The Committee recommends an updating of the poverty thresholds each year to reflect changes in median expenditure on food, clothing and shelter, a "conservative" updating procedure compared with linking with total consumption since it will tend to rise more rapidly than prices but less than total expenditure. The Committee argue that this is in line with the way subjective assessments of minimum income move over time, and may also be more acceptable to US policy-makers and the public than a complete switch to a purely relative approach. It is acknowledged that over a long enough period this will also lose touch with actual ordinary living standards, and a full-scale review every ten years is recommended.

The United Kingdom

The United Kingdom does not have an official poverty standard, nor does the government statistical apparatus produce estimates of the extent of poverty. However, there are officially-produced statistics relating to households on low incomes which are widely used in official and academic discussion of poverty. Up to 1988 the Department of Social Security (DSS, previously the DHSS), produced an annual series entitled "Low Income Families" (DSS, 1988a), showing the numbers with incomes below the safety net Supplementary Benefit support level, as well as those below 110 per cent, 120 per cent and 140 per cent of that level. The series was open to a number of criticisms (see Nolan, 1989; DSS, 1988b), the most fundamental being that use of social security rates as the (implicit poverty) standard gave rise to the anomalies already mentioned: raising support levels could increase measured poverty, and comparisons over time conflated changes in the generosity of the safety net with those in low incomes. In 1988 this series was discontinued and replaced by "Households Below Average Income" (HBAI — see DSS, 1988c), which shows the numbers and

types of households falling below both a set of thresholds calculated as proportions of average equivalent income and another
derived in that way for the base year but thereafter indexed in
line with prices only. One therefore gets a picture of the numbers
falling below both what are in effect relative income poverty lines
and below a range of income poverty lines held constant in real
terms from the base year.

While there are repeated official disclaimers about according
the figures the status of "poverty lines", public discussion has
tended to focus on those below half average income as "the poor"
The proportion of the population below half average income has
risen from 10 per cent in 1979 to 20 per cent in 1991/92.[6] Those
concerned with a fixed threshold, on the other hand, can highlight
the fact that there was a (small) fall in the proportion below half
average 1979 income uprated for inflation, with a larger fall in
the proportion below 60 per cent of that figure. The official HBAI
series extends back only to 1979, but Goodman and Webb (1994)
have applied the same methodology to FES data going back to
1961. This shows that the proportion of the population below half
average equivalent income fluctuated between 6-12 per cent from
1961 to 1985, then rose very sharply. Major changes in the composition of the households falling below that relative income line
have occurred, with a decline in the number in pensioner families
and an increase in the number in families with children, and with
unemployment becoming much more important as a cause of low
income (Goodman and Webb, 1994, p. A31).

The methodology used to construct the HBAI figures has been
reviewed and altered since its introduction, and the main areas of
concern illustrate the issues which arise in empirically implementing the apparently straightforward relative income line approach, or in monitoring progress *vis-à-vis* lines fixed in real
terms. Following the recommendations of the DSS Technical Review (1988b), moving to HBAI compared with the Low Income
Statistics involved a shift from the family/benefit unit to the
household as income recipient unit, from the equivalence scales
implicit in SB rates to those estimated from expenditure patterns

---

[6] See p. 37 and Table F1, DSS (1994). The HBAI series give results on the
basis of income both before and after housing costs; the figures quoted here
refer to before housing costs, which would be the most common usage internationally. With income after housing costs the proportion below half
average income rose even more, to about 25 per cent by 1991/92.

by McClements (1977),[7] and towards counting the number of individuals rather than families below income thresholds. An official "stocktaking" examination of the methodology of the HBAI series was carried out in 1991 (DSS, 1991) and some changes in the methodology were then implemented. Because of concerns that annual surveys may produce excessive year-to-year variation in incomes at the top and bottom of the distribution, it was decided to combine the results for two years in HBAI and to use information from income tax records (from the Inland Revenue's Survey of Personal Incomes) for the top of the distribution. Figures which are particularly sensitive to the equivalence scale used are identified as such. An appendix also shows where individuals would be located *vis-à-vis* the relative income thresholds if the benefit unit rather than the household was used as income recipient unit. Both the original technical review and the stocktaking exercise concluded that income was preferable to expenditure as the measure of living standards, primarily because expenditure as measured in the Family Expenditure Survey over a two-week period may fluctuate for reasons which do not reflect an underlying change in living standards. However, attention has been drawn to the anomalous position of some of those on very low incomes, who are seen to have relatively high expenditure and levels of possession of consumer durables (see also Davies 1994 and McGregor and Borooah, 1992).[8]

There has also been on-going debate about the use of the mean rather than the median in HBAI. From the outset, mean equivalent income across all households has been the yardstick from which income thresholds were derived, but initially means were also used to show how the incomes of different decile groups were evolving. For the bottom (and top) of the income distribution it was found that the mean was much less stable than the median from one year to another, being much more affected by outliers which could be due to sampling variation or misreporting. Since

---

[7] Equivalence scales provide a method of adjusting income for differences in household size and composition, incorporating a value for the "needs" of different household types relative to a benchmark type. For example, if a single adult counts as 1, an additional adult could count as 0.6 and each child as 0.4, this means that a couple with two children "needs" 2.4 times the income of a single adult to be at the same standard of living

[8] Davies (1994) shows that those at the very bottom of the income distribution have relatively high expenditure levels and levels of possession of certain consumer durables.

the second edition of HBAI, the median rather than the mean has therefore been shown for each decile group. The stocktaking report also considered whether the median rather than the mean for the entire distribution should be used as the benchmark for income thresholds. While noting the problem of the impact of outliers on the mean, the conclusion reached was that if the mean could be measured within an acceptable margin of error, it was preferable: the median and mean provide answers to different questions, and it is changes in position relative to the average for the population which are of greatest interest in this context[9]

The plethora of official statistics now published in the UK allows the user to arrive at conclusions which may differ depending on the extent to which they see poverty in primarily relative terms, which threshold is regarded as most appropriate, which adjustment for household size, which recipient unit, and so on. The underlying agnosticism is conveyed by the following quotation from the HBAI:

> Besides the questions of comprehensiveness, consistency and accuracy, one should bear in mind that HBAI results relate to a particular set of income definitions and methods for calculating income and deriving results. . . . It would have been possible to employ alternative definitions or methods, which in some cases might be as respectable and relevant as those actually employed. It can sometimes happen that alternative approaches give significantly different results. (DSS, 1992, pp. 9-10).

European Union

Research on poverty measurement sponsored by the Commission of the European Union and by Eurostat, the statistical office of the European Communities, has covered a considerable range. Cross-country studies have been carried out employing different approaches, including subjective income poverty lines and official minima, and the use of non-monetary indicators of poverty has also been explored recently. However, the main emphasis has been on relative income or expenditure lines, and it is on those lines that official statements about the level and trends in poverty in the Union have been based.

---

[9] DSS (1991) p. 13. The use of income before versus after housing costs in HBAI has also been extensively debated.

The Council of Ministers in 1975 defined the poor as "individuals or families whose resources are so small as to exclude them from the minimum acceptable way of life of the Member State in which they live". Thus poverty was seen as clearly relative, certainly across countries and presumably also over time since one could expect what constituted a "minimum acceptable way of life" to change as living standards in the country rose. Resources were central to the definition, and the notion of a common European standard, applying across all Member States, was implicitly rejected. The Final Report on the First Community Programme to Combat Poverty (Commission of the European Communities, 1981) sought to measure the extent of poverty in the different Member States by employing an income poverty line set at 50 per cent of average disposable equivalent income in the country in question. On this basis it was estimated that in the middle 1970s approximately 10 million households (11 per cent of the total), containing 30 million persons, were in poverty in the nine Member States of the then Community. However, the data and details of the way this procedure was applied differed across countries, seriously compromising comparability.[10]

The Second Poverty Programme, which ran from 1985 to 1989, took as its starting point the definition of poverty adopted in the Decision of the Council of Ministers of December 19, 1984:

> The poor shall be taken to mean persons, families and groups of persons whose resources (material, cultural and social) are so limited as to exclude them from the minimum acceptable way of life in the Member State in which they live.

Compared with the 1975 definition, lack of resources is now broadened to explicitly include cultural and social as well as material resources. Comparative poverty estimates for Member States and the Community as a whole for the early/mid-1980s were produced for the Commission as part of the Second Poverty Programme by O'Higgins and Jenkins (1990), and a separate set of studies were carried out for Eurostat. O'Higgins and Jenkins set out to measure poverty in the same way as the report on the

---

[10] This is amply demonstrated by the Irish example. No details were given in the Report as to how the figure for Ireland was produced or even the data source employed, and it has not been possible to reproduce it independently — see Nolan (1991).

First Programme, i.e., using proportions of national average income as the poverty line, but taking care to harmonise across countries as far as possible the data sources, definitions and methods of derivation of the estimates. They also looked at the numbers under 40 per cent and 60 per cent relative lines, and at the sensitivity of the results to the equivalence scale used. The "headline" result from their exercise, highlighted in various official Community documents, was that by 1985 the number of people below half average national income in then twelve Member States had risen to 44 million, compared with 38 million in 1975 and 40 million in 1980.[11]

The study *Poverty in Europe* carried out for Eurostat (ISSAS, 1990) again employed relative poverty lines but with household expenditure rather than income as the measure of resources, arguing that income definitions in surveys differed across countries and that the income data were often unreliable due to under-reporting, a serious problem for several countries (notably Greece). Poverty lines set at 40 per cent and 50 per cent of national average equivalent expenditure were applied. The use of the median rather than the mean was discussed, with the median seen as preferable since the mean is more sensitive to "extreme observations", but the mean was retained to conform with previous practice. The results showed that 50 million people, 15 per cent of the population of the Community, were below half the average for their country in the mid-1980s, and again this was widely referred to in official publications as the number in poverty at that date. The ISSAS study also estimated poverty rates for each country taking 50 per cent of average equivalent expenditure across the Community as a whole as the standard. The overall number in poverty is not then very different, but unsurprisingly the rates for the countries with relatively high average income or expenditure are lower and those for the poorer member states are much higher.

Within the Third Poverty Programme (which ran from 1990 to 1994), the microdata from the family budget surveys was brought together and directly analysed, by Hagenaars, de Vos and Zaidi (1994) to explore empirically the difference made by using income versus expenditure, alternative equivalence scales, and different

---

[11] While their overall figure for the mid-1970s for the then nine Member States was not very different to that in the Report on the First Programme, there were major but mostly offsetting differences for individual countries.

proportions of the average as threshold. They were also able to achieve greater consistency across countries than previous studies in the way income and expenditure were defined, and to reweight samples to improve their representativeness. Hagenaars et al., state clearly their theoretical preference for income as a measure of resources, and for a resource-based concept of poverty. However, because of underreporting in a number of Member States and possible measurement error in the survey income data, expenditure was considered to be the most reliable measure of resources for their set of countries. Their central results show 49 million persons living in households below half average equivalent expenditure in the country in question. Using a Community-wide rather than country-specific standard, 53 million persons are in households below half average equivalent expenditure, but 37 per cent of these live in the four poorest Member States, compared to 24 per cent of all those below the corresponding country-specific threshold.

The first (1994) Wave of the Europanel survey, the harmonised panel survey with common questionnaire and procedures which is being carried out for Eurostat in each Member State, of which the 1994 Living in Ireland Survey forms the Irish element, will make possible major improvements in the way poverty comparisons are made across community countries, particularly in the availability of a consistent microdata set. The availability of panel data from future waves will in addition provide a basis for the analysis of changes in poverty over time on a consistent basis, as well as the dynamics of income, labour force participation, household formation, etc., over time. Poverty analysis based on the panel will measure resources primarily in terms of income, since expenditure is not being measured in the survey in any depth, but a range of non-monetary indicators is also included, as discussed in Chapter 6 below. (As discussed in Section 2.2, the term social exclusion rather than poverty has come to dominate official EU usage; greater emphasis on non-monetary indicators may be seen as consistent with that trend, but using these indicators together with resources also provides an alternative way of measuring poverty as exclusion due to lack of resources.)

2.5 MEASURING POVERTY OVER TIME WITH SUMMARY POVERTY MEASURES

So far we have concentrated on how to identify the poor over time rather than on how best to summarise the extent of poverty — given a poverty line — in an aggregate measure. However, it is worth noting here that how one summarises the extent of poverty can also have important implications for the analysis of trends over time. Sen in a very influential paper (1976) highlighted the unsatisfactory features of the traditional head-count measure. One is that a transfer to someone just below the poverty line, bringing them just above the line, would reduce the head-count measure whereas the same transfer to a much needier person well below the line would have no impact. Another is that a transfer from someone just below the line to someone much worse off well below the line will also have no impact on the head-count. Sen proposed a summary measure which takes into account not only the number of people below the poverty line but also the depth of their poverty. Alternative measures which seek to do so have been put forward by, among others, Anand (1983), Thon (1979), Blackorby and Donaldson (1980), Clark, Hemming and Ulph (1981), and Foster, Greer and Thorbecke (1984) — a useful review is given by Foster (1984). Particular attention has been paid to setting out desirable features for such summary measures, and relating them to an underlying social welfare function. The family of measures proposed by Foster et al. has been shown by Foster and Shorrocks (1988a, b; 1991) to have some particularly attractive features, in terms both of its decomposition properties and its relationship with social welfare orderings, and will be employed in Chapter 4. The count of persons below income poverty lines will thus be complemented by measures which take into account the extent to which they fall below the line, opening up the possibility that one could observe an increase in the numbers counted as poor but a fall in the depth of their poverty, or vice versa.

2.6 CONCLUSIONS

This chapter has focused on the issues which have to be faced in seeking to measure poverty over time. It has critically reviewed the main approaches which have been used in developed countries in order to do so, and a discussion of official practice in three quite different settings — the USA, the UK and the European

Union — has helped to highlight many of the problems and choices involved. It has brought out the central choice to be made in applying monetary poverty lines over time, which is whether the poverty standard should be updated in line with prices or with average incomes in the society. The variation in official practice across the USA, UK and EU sums up the broader situation across developed countries: in the USA the official poverty line is indexed to prices, in the UK the official low income series use both thresholds held constant in real terms and ones linked to average income, and at EU level there has been an apparently little-questioned reliance on relative lines linked with average living standards in measuring changes over time (though the choice between country-specific or Community-wide lines has received attention).

The concept of poverty employed in this study is an explicitly relative one, relating to exclusion from the ordinary life of society due to lack of resources. We continue to stress, as in previous work, the importance of acknowledging uncertainty and absence of robustness in results where this exists. The application of a range of relative income lines, allowing the sensitivity of the results to the precise location of the line to be assessed, thus has clear advantages. While adhering firmly to a relative conception of poverty, we also see the value of supplementing such results with ones based on income thresholds held constant in real terms, so different perspectives can be adopted and the complete picture seen. This we see as being in the spirit of the approach advocated by Atkinson (1985; 1987) and Foster and Shorrocks (1988a), who argue that the diversity of possible judgements about the specification of the poverty line should be explicitly taken into account in the measurement procedures adopted. This general line of argument has been an important influence on recent poverty research internationally, with much more attention now being paid to the search for results which do not depend on — for example — precisely where the poverty line is set or how adjustment is made for household size.

This reinforces our long-standing belief that the most satisfactory general strategy to adopt is to present results using a range of income poverty lines and allow the reader to form his or her own judgements. (This undoubtedly gives rise to problems in conveying the overall picture to a broad audience, but these reflect the limits of our knowledge.) We also continue to explore the use of non-monetary indicators in poverty measurement, to focus

more firmly than income lines can do on those experiencing generalised deprivation due to lack of resources. Chapters 4, 5 and 6
apply income poverty lines and combined income plus deprivation
standards respectively to the 1994 data, showing how each can be
used to address the issues discussed in this chapter about measurement of changes in poverty over time. First, though, Chapter 3
provides a description of the 1994 Living in Ireland Survey and
the data it produced on which the study relies.

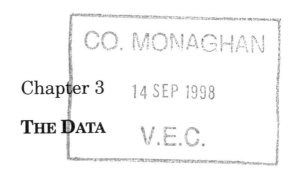

Chapter 3

THE DATA

3.1 INTRODUCTION

In this chapter we describe the 1994 Living in Ireland Survey and the data it produced, on which the study is based. We begin by considering in Section 3.2 the background to the survey, especially its links with the European Community Household Panel Survey (ECHP). Section 3.3 discusses the sample design and implications for subsequent reweighting of the data prior to analysis. Section 3.4 describes the fieldwork. Section 3.5 describes the structure and content of the questionnaires and the way they were administered. Section 3.6 sets out the response rates achieved at both the household and individual levels. A detailed description of the reweighting procedures adopted for the survey is presented in Section 3.7, while Section 3.8 looks at the representativeness of the data via detailed comparison of key variables in the sample with independent, external sources. An initial discussion of the income concept used in the current study is contained in Section 3.9, with further details in Chapter 4. Finally, Section 3.10 summarises the main points made in the course of the chapter.

3.2 BACKGROUND TO THE SURVEY

The idea of a pan-European panel survey was first mooted in the late 1980s. The objective of the project was to produce a fully harmonised dataset containing information on the economic, financial and other circumstances of households throughout the Union. This would initially cover the EU-12, with a view to expansion across the EU-15 as soon as feasible. The life of the panel was envisaged, at least in the first instance, to run over 1994, 1995 and 1996. The defining feature of the project is that it is based on a so-called longitudinal panel of households. This means that the *same* set of households will be interviewed in each of the three years in question. This methodology allows one to study changes in the characteristics and circumstance of particular households or household members over time. This longitudinal design contrasts with annually repeated cross-sections of the population in which a *new* sample of households would be selected each year for interview. The repeated cross-sectional approach provides information on net changes in a host of areas including income distribution, poverty, etc. It does not, however, allow one to examine the extent to which the circumstances of *individual* households change over time nor the processes and mechanisms underlying that change.

The key to realising the objective of a truly comparable data set across 12 different countries is harmonisation. Eurostat has ensured, as far as was possible, that all operational aspects of the project were centrally harmonised from Luxembourg. This included all aspects of data collection, coding, editing and data preparation. In addition, it also included harmonisation of the questionnaires in terms of their structure, content and interpretation. Eurostat issued a set of draft questionnaires for implementation in each Member State. The Living in Ireland Survey (which represents the Irish component of Eurostat's panel project) was built around these drafts. However, the Irish questionnaires used in the 1994 survey contained numerous additional modules and sets of questions which expanded on Eurostat's specifications.

Eurostat's drafts included two features worth noting at this point, which had an important influence on the structure of the Irish questionnaires. The first is a structural distinction in the individual questionnaire between those who worked 15 or more hours per week outside the home and those who did not. The former group was classified as economically active, the latter as inactive. This distinction can be considered as structural in the extent to which it determined much of the respondent's subsequent routing and classification through a large part of the remainder of the individual questionnaire. The 15-hour per week threshold is entirely specific to the European Community Household Panel Survey and does not conform to European Labour Force or ILO classifications. By building on Eurostat's drafts of the questionnaires we were able to collect sufficient information on economic activity outside the home to allow us to redefine a number of less restrictive classifications of labour force status, including the Irish Labour Force Survey's Principal Economic Status which is largely self-defined by the respondent.

A second structural distinction of importance in the Eurostat drafts of the questionnaires relates to the income concept applied in data collection. Eurostat's main concern was with disposable income (i.e., gross income minus compulsory deductions for tax and Social Insurance contributions) *in the calendar year 1993*. Although one of Eurostat's data requirements was information on *current* employee income, all other income details were to be recorded in respect of calendar year 1993. This meant that the Eurostat draft questionnaires excluded current income receipts in respect of Social Welfare transfers, private pensions, etc. However, details on both current income receipts from these sources and receipts in 1993 were collected in the Irish version of the questionnaire. This allows us greater flexibility than provided by the Eurostat drafts to define current and/or annual income figures. Although the former is used exclusively throughout this report, the latter will be employed by Eurostat in its use of the ECHP data for Ireland; the differences between the two will be explored in subsequent research.

A particularly important aspect of the project where complete harmonisation was not possible was sample design and selection procedures. This was entirely due to differences between Member States in the availability of population lists. Some countries, notably Denmark, have so-called population registers. These involve each member of the national population having a unique identification number and corresponding record in the national population register file. These identifiers are used for tax and social insurance purposes, welfare payments, etc. The fact that everyone in the national population is recorded in the registers (which are updated on an ongoing basis) provides a near perfect sampling frame for selecting samples at both the individual and household levels. In Britain, researchers have access to a computer-based file containing the postal address of almost every household in England, Scotland and Wales. This postal address file (PAF) also constitutes a near perfect frame for selecting samples of households. As discussed in Section 3.3 below, the sampling frame used in Ireland was the Register of Electors. This provides a listing of all adults over 18 years of age who are registered to vote in Dáil, Local Government or European Parliament Elections.

Given these variations in the origin of the population lists across Member States, sample design was possibly the aspect of the project which was least harmonised by Eurostat. Although harmonisation *per se* was difficult to implement at sample design stage, all selection procedures were submitted in advance for vetting by Eurostat. All samples used in the European Household Panel Survey were probabilistic, that is, statistical rather than quota sampling was employed. A related technical aspect of survey implementation is the reweighting procedures used to ensure representativeness of the data. To the extent that these must reflect sample design it was inevitable that completely harmonised procedures could not be implemented (given that sample design procedures differed from one country to another). Notwithstanding these differences, however, Eurostat issued a set of guidelines and criteria which the reweighting procedures had to meet. Indeed, Eurostat itself undertook the task of reweighting the data for the majority of Members States, in line with the relevant sample design procedures of the country in question. In Ireland, the ESRI undertook all aspects of reweighting in line with the harmonised criteria issued by Eurostat, as discussed in detail in Section 3.7 below.

3.3 SAMPLE DESIGN

The objective of the sample design was to obtain a representative sample of private households in Ireland. Those living in institutions — mostly long-term hospital patients and those in prison — were excluded from the target population. This exclusion is in line with the harmonised guidelines set down by Eurostat and is in keeping with the standard practice adopted in surveys of this nature, notably the Household Budget Survey conducted by the Irish Central Statistics Office. The 1991 Census of Population showed that 3,433,048 persons out of the total population of 3,525,719 lived in private households. This means that our target population covered just over 97 per cent of all persons in the State. As well as the institutional population, the 3 per cent of the population excluded from the target population also include people who are homeless and Travellers not living in permanent households. These are small groups but ones which face a relatively high risk of poverty. However, a general survey such as the present one is not in any case appropriate for the study of such groups, which require very particular research methodologies.[1]

---

[1] Reliance on the Electoral Register also means that the very small number of households comprising only individuals aged under 18 are omitted.

Because the electoral register is a list of *electors* the target sample which was selected was effectively a sample of *persons*, not *households*. The sample was selected using the ESRI's RANSAM system, which is based on stratification of District Electoral Divisions (Whelan, 1979; Keogh and Whelan, 1986), and the precise way in which this was done is described in detail in Appendix 1. The target sample was selected as 259 clusters, each of 28 respondents, giving a total of 7,252. As discussed in Section 3.5 below, we attempted to interview all adults in the household of those included in the target sample. Since larger households have a higher probability of selection than smaller ones, the sample will over-represent larger households, which has implications for reweighting the sample taken up in Section 3.7 below. While the Electoral Register has some less-than-ideal features as a sampling frame, as discussed in Appendix 1, Keogh and Whelan (1986) concluded that it:

> ... is the best generally available frame from which samples of the Irish population may be selected. While it does contain some bias against young people and recent movers, this is unlikely to be serious except where the variable of interest is powerfully affected by age or recency of moving (p. 91).

They also show that the register is a relatively complete listing of the usually resident population and concurs well with Census data on total population numbers within each district.

3.4 FIELDWORK

Planning for the Irish component of the European Community Household Panel Survey began in late 1991 and ran throughout 1992. A two-wave pilot was carried out in each of the then 12 Member States in 1993. The pilot in Ireland was carried out in March and November 1993 on an initial target panel of 200 households. The final effective sample of households at the end of the second wave of the pilot was 118. This two-phase pilot was used to test the feasibility of simultaneously administering a harmonised questionnaire to a panel of households in each Member State as well as developing and testing the contents of the questionnaires themselves. In addition, the pilot was used to design the coding and editing protocols, and to develop software to check the internal consistency of the data files and to reformat them in a consistent and harmonised fashion throughout all Member States for subsequent analysis by Eurostat.

Fieldwork for the first round of the main survey was carried out in Ireland throughout the Summer and Autumn of 1994. A total of 121 interviewers worked at some point on the survey. A personalised letter was sent to each respondent selected from the Electoral Register in advance of the initial approach by the interviewer. This provided some details on the background to the survey as well as outlining its content and to whom the interviewer would like to speak when she (all were women) visited the household. Each household was also sent a brochure which contained information on the survey, discussing in some detail its content and issues of confidentiality, etc. A lottery "scratch card" was given to each individual who completed the individual questionnaire. Interviewers were instructed to make a minimum of four call-backs to each household in an attempt to make initial contact with its members before the household was dropped from the sample and classified as unavailable.[2] The households which participated in the survey often required multiple visits by the interviewer to complete all individual questionnaires. The average number of visits per *completed* household was 2.9, with a minimum of 1 and a maximum of 16. All interviews were conducted on a personally administered (rather than self-completion) basis.

3.5 UNIT OF DATA COLLECTION AND QUESTIONNAIRES

There were two distinct data collection units employed in the survey, namely the household and the individual adult. Following the widely-accepted definition, a private household was defined as a group of persons who live together, share some form of communal "kitty" or other budgeting arrangement and usually meet together at least once each week for a common meal.[3] Within each household the interviewer attempted to administer a *household questionnaire* to the "Household Reference Person" or their spouse. Following Eurostat guidelines, the "Household Reference Person" was defined as the owner or tenant of the accommodation

---

[2] No substitution of households was allowed.

[3] This does not necessarily entail assuming that everyone in the household shares a common standard of living: the unit of *analysis* to be employed is discussed in Chapter 4.

or, in cases of joint ownership or tenancy, the older of the two or more persons who were equally responsible for the accommodation. In the event, about three-quarters of the individuals identified as household reference person in this manner were male. Where the household reference person was one of a married couple (both living in the household), in about 94 per cent of cases this procedure resulted in the man being the reference person.

The second data collection unit was each member of the household who was *born in 1977 or earlier* — and so was at least 16 years of age in the year of interview. The interviewer attempted to administer a detailed personal interview to each such member of the household. Finally, in households where there was a farm the interviewer completed a dedicated farm questionnaire with the person in charge of the farm or the person who did most work on it.

The Household Register and Household Questionnaire

The purpose of the household questionnaire was to collect details on characteristics of the household in general. The first section of the questionnaire contained the household roster or register. This was used to record information on who actually lived in the household; their dates of birth; the inter-relationship of each member to each other member; whether or not each member was currently resident and, if not, the reason for his/her temporary absence;[4] their eligibility for interview and outcome code for completion or otherwise of the individual questionnaire. This register formed the backbone of the survey as it provided a complete picture of who was in the household, who should be interviewed etc.[5]

In addition to the register the household questionnaire collected information on the following areas:

1. The length of time the household had been at their current address and their reason for moving to that address.

---

[4] It is possible for someone to be a member of a household but to be currently absent on a temporary basis, e.g., someone who is temporarily in hospital; temporarily working away from home; temporarily away from home in full-time education, etc.

[5] Given the longitudinal nature of the project the household register will be particularly important in tracking changes in household membership between one phase and the next.

2. The number of rooms and general facilities available to the household.

3. The household's perception of its immediate environs in terms of a number of proxies of socio-economic well-being.

4. Details on the nature of ownership or tenancy along with ongoing cost of same.

5. Information on a wide range of items or activities available to the household. (The manner in which some of these can be employed as non-monetary indicators of deprivation is discussed in full in Chapter 6).

6. A range of questions on the household's ability to make ends meet, its sources and level of income, and perceived trends in its financial circumstances over the year preceding in the survey.

The Individual Questionnaire

This survey questionnaire was administered to *each member of the household born in 1977 or earlier*. Because the Living in Ireland Survey was harmonised around the European Community Household Panel Survey, as already noted this questionnaire was built around an important structural distinction between those who worked for 15 hours or more outside the home each week and those who did not. For routing purposes the former group was considered to be economically active, the latter to be inactive. The individual questionnaire contained eleven main sections covering the following areas:

A. Detailed information on the employment situation of those *who worked outside the home for at least 15 hours per week* and on current income from that employment.

B. Details on the activity of persons who were defined as being economically inactive along with information on education or training currently being undertaken (if any) and the reason for the respondent's current economic inactivity.

C. Details on the nature of work undertaken in the week preceding the survey by those respondents whose principal economic status was economically inactive, along with information on the income from that work. The reader should note that many persons who are retired, on home duties, etc., may hold a job outside the home for a few hours per week. It was details of this job which were collected in this section of the questionnaire.

D. Information from those who were economically inactive on job search activity and reservation wages.

E. Details on the last *main* job or business (defined as being 15 or more hours each week) undertaken by those whose principal economic status was inactive.

F. Details from all respondents on daily activity and behaviour including, for example, amount of time spent caring for children or others in need of special attention; patterns of socialisation; attitudes to social and State institutions including political affiliations.

G. General information on training or education undertaken over the period from the beginning of January 1993 to the date of interview as well as a month by month record of principal economic status over the same period.

(There was no sections H or I to avoid confusion with the household questionnaire).

J. Details on various sources of income in the calendar year of 1993. These sources of income included; from work as an employee; as a non-agricultural self-employed person; as a farmer; from casual or secondary employment; from transfers through the Social Welfare system (including Child Benefit); from interest or dividends on bank, building society deposits, etc., stocks or shares, unit-linked funds, etc.; from occupational or other private pension schemes; from trade union or sick pay; from annuities, covenants or trusts; from private or charitable transfers (including regular financial assistance from charities, alimony and maintenance payments, etc.); from educational grants. In the case of social welfare transfers, full details on current receipts were also obtained.

K. Details of regular payments throughout 1993 which were made by the individual in respect of items such as voluntary health insurance, private pensions, direct payment of Social Insurance and Health Contributions, direct tax payments to the Revenue Commissioners, etc.

L. Information on physical health status and on use of the health services.

M. Biographical and life history details including date of birth; marital status; place of birth; age on taking up first regular job; level of educational attainment; vocational training completed; occupational and educational attainment of respondent's parents; proxies on the respondent's current level of psychological well-being and general outlook on life (these latter two sections of the questionnaire are used to construct indices of psychological distress and fatalism).

The Farm Questionnaire

A dedicated farm questionnaire was administered (where relevant) to collect information on farm size; agricultural area utilised; acreage under a range of different types of crops; yield per acre; type of cattle or pig production (where relevant); labour input to the farm and headage premia, subsidies and transfers to the farm. The information recorded in the farm questionnaire was principally used to assign each farm to the international Farm Accounts Data Network (FADN) classification system. In addition to this information, the interviewer also marked the location of the farm on an Ordnance Survey map. This was subsequently used to classify each farm according to its principal soil type. Using detailed family farm income coefficients provided by Teagasc (the Agriculture and Food Development Authority), we were able to make an estimate of the family farm income for each farm based on its soil type, farm system and size. The reference year in respect of which information on level of farm activity was collected was 1993, the last completed full year of activity preceding the survey.

3.6 RESPONSE RATES

Household Level Response

Table 3.1 presents details on the household-level response outcomes from the survey. As we have seen, the initial target sample consisted of 7,252 households, selected as 259 clusters each of 28 households. In the course of fieldwork a total of 166 of these households were identified as being invalid elements of the population in the sense that they did not constitute a current, private household: 91 were identified as being institutions, and in the remaining 75 the individual selected had been living alone and was now deceased. Excluding these elements left us with a valid target sample of 7,086 households for interview. From section 4 of the table we can see that contact was not made with 609 households. Of these, 450 had moved address since registering on the electoral list, a further 45 addresses had been demolished and a total of 114 addresses could not be located by the interviewer.[6] This means that we were able to contact a total of 6,477 valid addresses, representing an address contact rate of 91.4 per cent.

.Section 6 of the table shows that we did not achieve a successful interview with 2,429 of the households which were contacted. This means that 37.5 per cent of valid addresses which were contacted were not interviewed. Of these 1,824 were due to straightforward refusal (28.2 per cent of the total). The total number of households which were successfully interviewed was 4,048, representing 62.5 per cent of the valid addresses contacted. The overall household response rate (as a percentage of the valid target sample) was 57.1 per cent. This level of household response rate is much as one would expect in an intensive survey of this nature. The comparable figure for the 1987 Household Budget Survey carried out by the Central Statistics Office is 58 per cent.[7]

---

[6] In many other cases the target household had moved from the address given on the electoral register but had been successfully located at a new address by the interviewer.

[7] This figure relates to the 11,802 "non-farm" households which participated in full with the 1987 HBS. The additional 1,036 "farm" households which participated in the 1987 HBS were taken from Teagasc's National Farm Survey (1987). The fact that this farming subgroup were established respondents in Teagasc's panel of farm households resulted in a substantial upward bias in their response rates. Consequently, they must be excluded in calculating overall response rates. For a full discussion of response rates in the 1987 HBS, see Appendix 4 of *Household Budget Survey, 1987*, Vol. 1, Stationery Office, December 1987.

TABLE 3.1: HOUSEHOLD RESPONSE OUTCOMES, PHASE 1 (1994) OF
LIVING IN IRELAND SURVEY

1. Target Sample	7,252	
2. Invalid Elements of which: Deceased Institutions	166 75 91	
3. Valid Target Sample	7,086	
4. Non-contact of which: Moved, No forwarding address Demolished, No forwarding address Unable to locate address	609 450 45 114	Percentage of Valid Addresses Contacted
5a. Valid Addresses Contacted	6,477	100.0%
5b. Address Contact Rate (5a/3)	91.4%	
6. Not Interviewed of which: Ill/Senile Temporarily Absent Not Available Other Refusal	2,429 121 25 303 156 1,824*	37.5% 1.9% 0.4% 4.7% 2.4% 28.2%
7. Interviewed	4,048	62.5%
8. Overall Household Response Rate (7/3)	57.1%	

* This includes a total of 130 households which were partially completed in
the field but which were not included for analysis due either to a substantial degree of unit non-response or item non-response on the key income
questions

When the initial phase of interviewing had been completed in the
1994 round of the survey we undertook a so-called "refusal
conversion" exercise. This involved sending a core group of
interviewers to 530 households which had initially refused to
participate in the survey when first approached by an interviewer.
The 530 households in question were selected from the clusters
with the lowest response rates after initial interviewing had been
completed. The response rate for this conversion exercise was 25
per cent (133 households) successfully completed. This refusal
conversion exercise is reflected in the figures presented in Table
3.1.

Individual Level Response

A total of 14,583 persons were members of the 4,048 households which were successfully interviewed in the 1994 round of the survey. Of these a total of 10,411 were eligible for personal interview (i.e. born in 1977 or earlier). A total of 9,905 eligible respondents successfully completed the full individual questionnaire (964 on a proxy basis). This means that 506 eligible members of these households who should have completed an individual questionnaire failed to do so. Provision was made within the household questionnaire to collect some summary details in respect of these non-respondents. Information on their level of educational attainment, principal economic status, and main sub-aggregates of income were collected in the Summary Sheet at the end of the household questionnaire. The information contained in this summary sheet, along with date of birth and interrelationship codes, allowed us to integrate these so-called unit non-respondents[8] into the full data file of individual-level questionnaires. By so doing we were able to calculate an estimate for each household's total income. The 506 unit non-respondents represents just under 5 per cent of all eligible members within responding households. This is a low level of internal non-response in a survey of this nature. We achieved complete internal response in 90 per cent of responding households. In a further 8 per cent we had one non-respondent and in the remaining 2 per cent of completed households we had two non-respondents. Households with more than two non-respondents were counted as refusals.[9]

3.7 REWEIGHTING THE DATA

Survey samples can be adversely affected by bias from a number of sources. The two most important are bias resulting from sample design effects and bias resulting from differential non-response among various subgroups in the target sample. To ensure the representativeness of the data it is necessary to adjust the composition of the sample to eliminate any identifiable bias which

---

[8] A *unit* non-respondent within a household is an eligible member who does not complete an individual questionnaire. This contrasts with item non-response which refers to non-response of a specific question (or item) in an otherwise completed individual questionnaire (or unit).

[9] In Table 3.1, such households are among the 130 mentioned in the note.

may have arisen from either of these two sources. This is achieved
by reweighting the data so as to ensure that the structure of the
sample (according to certain key classificatory variables which are
known to be particularly important in terms of one's research
objectives) correspond with the known structure of the population
as derived from external independent sources. In other words, we
look at what percentage of households in the sample fall into
certain classificatory groups and compare this with the percentage of households in the population which fall into the same
groups. The greater the difference between the structure of the
effective sample and population the greater is the potential non-
representativeness of the data. The external population figures
used in this comparison are usually derived from sources such as
the Labour Force Survey or the Census of Population.

Potential bias due to sample design could arise from use of the
Electoral Register as sampling frame. As noted in Section 3.2, the
register is not a perfect population list. In particular, the most
important source of bias lies in the fact that large households
have a higher probability of selection than small ones, so this
must be directly addressed by the reweighting procedure. One
also generally finds that households in rural areas have a higher
propensity to participate in sample surveys than do those in
urban areas, especially in Dublin. In the 1994 round of the Living
in Ireland Survey we found a crude[10] response rate of 64 per cent
in rural areas, 56 per cent in urban areas outside Dublin, and 46
per cent in Dublin. Because of these substantial variations in
regional response rates it is also important to have an explicit
regional dimension in the reweighting scheme. Differential
response by characteristics such as age, social class or employment status could also be important in the context of studying
poverty.

The final reweighting scheme adopted is described in full in
Appendix 2, but the main elements are outlined here. It had three
distinct steps, as follows:

Step 1: Adjustment for Farm Households.

Among farm households the response rate for small farmers is
substantially lower than that of large farmers. Consequently, in
the first step of reweighting we adjusted the sample structure of

---

[10] By *crude* we refer to the rates before adjusting for deadwood or other
ineligible elements in the population list.

farming households in line with the population structure derived from the Census of Agriculture.

Step 2: Weights Adjusting the Distribution of Households

In this step we adjusted the distribution of households in the effective sample with reference to independent population estimates provided by the Central Statistics Office in the form of detailed cross-tabulations from the 1993 Labour Force Survey. (The 1994 LFS was not available at the stage the weights were being developed.) A five-way weighting matrix was used, based on the number of adults in the household, the number of persons at work, socio-economic group, age and location.

Step 3: Weights Correcting for the Distribution of Persons

The third step in the weighting procedure involved using the weight derived in the first two steps to adjust for the distribution of *persons*. To do this we assigned the *household*-level weight of Steps 1 and 2 to each *individual* in the sample. Having done this we were able to derive a weighted sample distribution of *persons* according to sex, age and marital status. The same distribution of *persons* was extracted from the 1993 Labour Force Survey. Ratio weights were then derived on the basis of the population and weighted sample distributions so as to bring the latter into line with the former. Household and individual weights were then re-estimated using an iterative procedure. While the final household level weights produced by Step 3 were not very different to those produced by Steps 1 and 2, this step does allow us to address any potential bias arising from the underrepresentation of young single households on the Electoral Register.

3.8 VALIDATING THE SAMPLE DATA

Having carried out the reweighting procedure one must assess the representativeness of the data with reference to known population distributions derived from independent, external sources. The most important sources for validation purposes include the 1994 Labour Force Survey, the 1991 Census of Population and the administrative statistics on Social Welfare recipiency rates published by the Department of Social Welfare. Table 3.2 presents a comparison of the distributions of persons classified by age and marital status derived from the weighted sample and the Labour Force Survey. One can see that there are

only minimal differences between the two distributions. Table 3.3
compares a breakdown of persons classified by age and sex from
the weighted sample with that derived from the 1991 Census of
Population. Once again there are only minimal differences
between the population and sample distributions. The greatest
difference (of 1 percentage point) is for females in the 25-34 age
cohort. The overall split between males and females is virtually
identical from both sources. Such differences as exist are clearly
attributable to sampling variability.

TABLE 3.2: DISTRIBUTIONS OF PERSONS CLASSIFIED BY AGE AND
MARITAL STATUS FROM LIVING IN IRELAND SURVEY (LII) 1994 AND
LABOUR FORCE SURVEY (LFS) 1994

Marital Status		% in Age Cohort (years)							Column %
		15-24	25-34	35-44	45-54	55-64	65+	Total	
Single	LII	60.3	18.0	6.0	4.1	3.9	7.7	100.0	38.8
	LFS	57.1	19.9	6.6	4.3	4.2	7.8	100.0	39.0
Married	LII	1.3	20.4	28.1	22.6	14.8	12.8	100.0	51.8
	LFS	1.3	20.1	28.0	22.8	14.8	13.1	100.0	51.5
Separated*	LII	0.0	21.0	36.8	26.3	10.5	5.3	100.0	2.2
	LFS	0.6	18.3	35.9	28.0	11.6	5.6	100.0	2.4
Widowed	LII	0.0	1.1	2.6	5.8	16.9	73.5	100.0	7.2
	LFS	0.0	0.7	2.1	6.1	15.5	75.6	100.0	7.2
Total	LII	24.1	18.1	17.9	14.3	10.6	15.0	100.0	100
	LFS	22.9	18.6	18.0	14.5	10.6	15.3	100.0	100

* Includes divorced.
Source: Living in Ireland Survey, Labour Force Survey, Table 5.

Tables 3.4 and 3.5 consider some household characteristics which
are particularly relevant in the context of income distribution,
poverty and deprivation. Table 3.4 compares the sample and
Labour Force Survey distributions of households cross-classified
by the number of persons whose principal economic status is "At
Work" and the number of persons who are unemployed. There is
very little difference between the two distributions. The total
number of unemployed individuals defined in terms of principal

TABLE 3.3: DISTRIBUTIONS OF PERSONS CLASSIFIED BY AGE AND
SEX FROM 1991 CENSUS OF POPULATION AND LIVING IN IRELAND
SURVEY 1994

Age Cohort	Males		Females	
	Census 1991	LII 1994	Census 1991	LII 1994
	(Per Cent)			
0-4	8.0	8.2	7.5	7.7
5-14	19.5	19.5	18.3	19.1
15-24	17.6	18.0	16.6	16.9
25-34	13.9	13.1	14.2	13.2
35-44	13.3	13.1	13.0	12.9
45-54	10.0	10.5	9.6	10.2
55-64	7.8	7.9	7.9	7.6
65+	9.9	9.6	12.9	12.2
Total	100	100	100	100
% of all persons	49.7	49.2	50.3	50.8

TABLE 3.4: DISTRIBUTION OF HOUSEHOLDS CROSS-CLASSIFIED BY
NUMBER OF PERSONS AT WORK AND NUMBER OF PERSONS
UNEMPLOYED, LII SURVEY AND LABOUR FORCE SURVEY (LFS) 1994

No. of Persons At Work		No. of Persons Unemployed (incl. first job Seekers)			
		None	1	2+	Total
		(Per Cent)			
None	LII	73.1	21.2	5.7	100.0
	LFS	73.9	21.9	4.2	100.0
1	LII	86.2	12.1	1.8	100.0
	LFS	87.2	11.1	1.7	100.0
2 or more	LII	91.4	7.3	1.3	100.0
	LFS	92.0	6.8	1.2	100.0
Total	LII	83.1	13.9	3.0	100.0
	LFS	84.0	13.6	2.4	100.0

Source: Living in Ireland Survey, Labour Force Survey, Table 41.

economic status in the grossed-up survey is 220,000, very close to
the 218,000 shown by the Labour Force Survey.[11]

---

[11] Although the number of adults at work was included as a dimension in the
reweighting matrix in step 2 of the weighting procedure, the number of
persons unemployed was not.

Table 3.5 compares the numbers in receipt of the different
Social Welfare schemes as estimated from the grossed-up sample
with the 1994 administrative totals published by the Department
of Social Welfare. Looking first at pensions, we see that the
grossed-up estimate for receipt of Old Age (contributory or non-
contributory) or Retirement pension was 254,700 from the
sample, very close to the 256,616 total from administrative
records. However, the sample indicated that 91,700 persons were
in receipt of Survivors/Widow's/Widower's pensions compared
with Departmental figures of 109,700. It is relevant here that
there can be considerable confusion in the minds of recipients of
pensions about which specific scheme they are actually receiving,
and that the proportion of recipients living in institutions rather
than private households will be relatively high in the case of
pensions. Many respondents who are widowed and actually in
receipt of a Survivor's Pension may in fact believe that they are
receiving payment under an Old Age Contributory pension. While
every effort was made at the fieldwork and coding stages to
resolving such ambiguity, it is extremely difficult to eliminate it
completely. Adding the figures for Survivor's and Old
Age/Retirement Pensions one finds that the survey figure of
346,400 compares with a Departmental total of 366,316. As
approximately 8 per cent of the potential target population of
those eligible for pensions are in institutional care, however, the
total in private households consistent with the administrative
figure is about 340,000, very close to the grossed-up survey figure.

Table 3.5 shows that the grossed-up survey estimates for
Unemployment Benefit, Unemployment Assistance, Deserted
Wife's payments and Carer's Allowance are also very close to the
administrative totals. The numbers in the survey in receipt of
Lone Parent's Allowance are slightly higher than the administrative totals, at 45,500 compared with 40,700. The most substantial
divergence between the survey and administrative totals are for
sickness-related payments (Disability, Injury and Disablement
Benefits and Invalidity Pension) and for Supplementary Welfare
Allowance. The total in receipt of sickness-related schemes in the
grossed-up sample is 73,400, well below the administrative total
of 92,800. The explanation for this under-representation is not
obvious, though it may reflect difficulty in obtaining a response
from some ill individuals — a similar level of under-
representation was seen for this group in the 1987 ESRI survey.
Finally, administrative figures show about 16,800 recipients

of regular weekly payments under Supplementary Welfare Allowance (SWA) in 1994. The survey sought to distinguish between regular weekly SWA payments, additional regular payments for special factors such as heating or diet, and once-off exceptional needs payments. The grossed-up survey total for basic weekly payments is only 2,400 recipients. Even taking into account possible confusion by respondents of the different types of SWA payment, the survey total for all three types of payment was still only about 8,500. This group was well represented in the 1987 survey, and changes in the questionnaire format may have contributed to its under-representation in 1994.[12]

TABLE 3.5: NUMBER OF RECIPIENTS OF MAJOR SOCIAL WELFARE PAYMENTS BASED ON ADMINISTRATIVE FIGURES AND ESTIMATES FROM LII 1994

Scheme Type	LII 1994	Department of Social Welfare, 1994
Old Age and Retirement*	254,700	256,616
Unemployment Benefit	61,400	62,909
Unemployment Assistance	203,200	206,525
Sickness Payments**	73,400	92,834
Widow's/Widower's Pension	91,700	109,700
Lone Parent's Allowance	45,500	40,700
Deserted Wife's Benefit/Allowance	15,900	15,700
Carer's Allowance	5,300	5,100

* Includes Social Welfare Retirement Pension; Old Age Contributory and Non-Contributory Pensions; Pre-retirement Allowance; Pro-Rata Mixed Insurance Pension.

**Includes Disability Benefit, Invalidity Pension; Injury Benefit; Disablement Benefit

Source: Administrative figures are taken from Statistical Information on Social Welfare Services, 1994, Stationery Office, Dublin 1995.

It is worth adverting at this point to the recent study by the CSO on the differences between the Labour Force Survey estimates of unemployment and the Live Register. We saw above that the

---

[12] In 1987 SWA was covered by a separate question, whereas in 1994 it was included in the broader question about receipt of social welfare and came at the end of a lengthy list of schemes.

Living in Ireland Survey produces an estimate for the total
number unemployed which is very close to the Labour Force
Survey figure for April 1994, of about 220,000. In both these
surveys — and throughout this study — the measure of unemployment is based on the way the respondent describes his or her
labour market activity. Whether the individual is signing on the
Live Register, or is receiving unemployment benefit or assistance,
does not enter into the measurement of unemployment. The
measure of unemployment, and of labour force status more
generally, used here is not therefore directly affected by the
findings of the CSO study that some of those known to be on the
Live Register reported in the Labour Force Survey that they were
employed — that is, some people are "working and claiming".[13] We
have also seen that the Living in Ireland Survey provides
estimates of the numbers in receipt of UB and UA which are very
close to administrative totals. If some of those on the Live
Register (other than those legitimately working and claiming
because they are, for example, on systematic short-time) report
themselves as at work rather than in receipt of unemployment
compensation in surveys such as the LFS or the Living in Ireland
Survey, one might in fact expect those surveys to underestimate
the numbers in receipt. The LFS does ask whether respondents
are on the Live Register and whether they are in receipt of UA or
UB, but this information was not covered in the published CSO
study. This is clearly an issue requiring further research, both
using the LFS and the Living in Ireland Survey. For the present,
we will take its implications into account by assessing the
sensitivity of our key results in Chapter 4 to the possible extent of
working and claiming via simulation methods.

As far as the representativeness of the income figures derived
from the survey are concerned, the most directly comparable
figure will be from the 1994 Household Budget Survey (HBS),
which has not been published at time of writing. There are
methodological and definitional differences between the income
concepts derived from the survey and those available from either
the Revenue Commissioner's Annual Reports or the National
Accounts which make it difficult to assess the income aggregates
in the survey. However, when we come to the analysis of changes

---

[13] The CSO study does not allow a straightforward estimate of the extent of
working and claiming, for a variety of reasons which will not be detailed
here.

in average income between the 1987 and 1994 surveys in Chapter 4, comparison will be made with external information from the National Accounts and CSO data on average earnings.

3.9 THE INCOME MEASURE

As discussed in Section 3.5, the questionnaires collected information on a wide range of income types, both in respect of current income receipts and also in respect of calendar year 1993. Details were collected on both current and 1993 income from the following sources: employment as an employee; self-employment; farming; secondary jobs; casual employment; State training or work experience schemes; Social Welfare transfers; Child Benefit; the renting of land or property, etc.; interest or dividends from all forms of deposit accounts; unit linked funds; stocks and shares and similar such financial instruments; retirement pensions; pensions from abroad; annuities, covenants or trusts; sick pay from an employer; trade union strike or sick pay; private or charitable maintenance from outside the household (including alimony payments); educational grants.

For most sources of income, such as earnings, Social Welfare transfers, and private pensions, details were recorded in respect of the amount received in the current pay period (week, fortnight, month, etc.). A longer reference period was used for certain other income sources, because it would not be very meaningful to collect details on current weekly or monthly receipts in respect of income from self-employment, farming, property rental or investment income. In respect of these income sources details were recorded on the basis of the most recently available annual figures (in nearly all cases, details were provided in respect of 1993). The information used in our estimation of farm income was also collected in respect of 1993. Such incomes recorded on an annual basis were converted to a weekly average for the analysis.

The income details collected allow one to derive various income concepts. In the present report we present income information and related poverty lines based on the concept of current disposable income. This is defined as gross income minus compulsory deductions of income tax, health and social insurance payments. All other deductions, including superannuation contributions, Trade Union subscriptions, life insurance premia, VHI subscriptions, regular savings or mortgage repayments deducted by the employer at source from gross pay, etc., were added back to the net take-home pay to provide our measure of disposable income. Income from self-employment is net profit after deducting all expenses and wages to staff but before deducting money drawn out of the business for private or domestic purposes. The farm income measure is family farm income derived from the farm in 1993, which comes closest to the non-agricultural self-employment income concept. As discussed in Section 3.5 above, farm income was estimated indirectly on the basis of information on output and stocking levels which was collected in a dedicated questionnaire administered to farm households, in conjunction with soil type and detailed family farm income coefficients provided by Teagasc to make estimates of annual farm income arising from agricultural activity. The income definitions employed are in line with those adopted by the CSO in the Household Budget Survey. We discuss in Chapter 4 the implications of adopting this income definition for the analysis of low income and poverty.

3.10 SUMMARY

We began this chapter by discussing the background to the survey, particularly its links to the European Community Household Panel Survey. By any standard the European Community Household Panel project is an extremely ambitious undertaking, with enormous potential as the basis for policy-relevant research. The strength of the complete European dataset lies not only in the amount and richness of detail provided on each Member State as a separate national entity, but in the fact that it is fully harmonised across countries. In addition, the panel or longitudinal nature of the project will offer the opportunity to study changes and dynamics in the circumstances and character-istics of households or individuals at both country and EU level. The European project was particularly timely in Ireland as it provided an unrivalled opportunity to update and extend the knowledge-base built up from the household survey carried out by the ESRI in 1987. By adding various sections and modules to the core questionnaires we have been able to generate an even more valuable dataset. This study is intended to be the first of many to draw on the information collected in the survey.

This chapter outlined operational aspects of the project such as sample design, fieldwork and the content of the questionnaires used at the level of the household, the individual and the farm. It also considered response rates, technical aspects of reweighting the data and subsequent validation. We saw that the household response rate was 62.5 per cent while within these households the individual response rate was 95 per cent (including proxies). Given the extremely onerous nature of the questionnaires used and the relative sensitivity of many of the issues discussed (notably income) these response rates compare favourably with similar such surveys which focus on family income or expenditure.

The data validation indicates that the reweighted sample adequately represents the population according to key variables such as principal economic status, age, sex, and numbers in receipt of social welfare. The numbers unemployed, measured using respondent's descriptions of their labour force activity, are close to those produced in the same manner by the CSO's Labour Force Survey. The implications for our key results of the possible extent of working full-time while claiming unemployment compensation, highlighted by the recent CSO study of the Labour Force Survey and the Live Register, will be considered at the relevant point in Chapter 4. The disposable income concept used throughout this report corresponds to the concept adopted by the CSO in its Household Budget Survey as well as similar such surveys which are undertaken elsewhere, for example in the Family Expenditure Survey carried out in the United Kingdom. In Chapter 4, this income measure provides the basis for the analysis of income poverty in Ireland in 1994.

Chapter 4

INCOME POVERTY: AGGREGATE RESULTS AND TRENDS

4.1 INTRODUCTION

The discussion of concepts and measures of poverty in Chapter 2 indicated the value of using a number of approaches to poverty measurement in order to shed light on the extent and nature of poverty. The programme of poverty research carried out using the 1987 ESRI Survey has demonstrated the practical value of such a strategy. It can help to identify results on the characteristics of poor households, and trends in poverty over time, which do not depend on obtaining precise agreement as to the location of the poverty line. A similar strategy is therefore being adopted in analysing the new database for 1994.

We begin in this chapter, by examining aggregate measures of poverty based wholly on income information. Chapter 5 goes on to examine the distribution of poverty over households of different types based on relative income poverty lines, and how this has changed over time. Information on non-income indicators of deprivation is explored and combined with income information to produce alternative measures of poverty in Chapter 6, which can be compared with results for 1987 using the same approach (Callan, Nolan, and Whelan, 1993, 1994; Nolan and Whelan, 1996).

In this chapter, the relative income poverty line approach is applied to the data for 1994. A major advantage of this approach is that it allows us to extend our earlier analysis of trends in relative income poverty between 1973 and 1987 up to the 1990s. In doing so, we use measures which reflect not only how many people have incomes below the relevant cut-off, but also the "depth of income poverty" they experience — how great the gap is between their incomes and the poverty line defined by the relative income cut-off.

Since changes in the extent and nature of poverty between
1987 and 1994 are the central concern of this study, we begin by
sketching out in Section 4.2 the way key macroeconomic
aggregates and social welfare rates have evolved over this period.
Section 4.3 sets out the methodological considerations which arise
in applying income poverty lines in the present context. Section
4.4 presents the basic results for 1994, showing how the head
counts of poverty on a household and individual basis vary with
the level of the cut-off and the equivalence scale employed.
Section 4.5 compares the key results for 1994 with 1987. Trends
in aggregate poverty measures over a longer period, of the last 20
years, are examined in Section 4.6. In assessing trends in income
poverty over time, the limitations of simple "head count"
measures are stressed, and alternative measures which take into
account the depth of poverty are presented. Section 4.7 draws
together the main results and brings out some of their implications.

4.2 THE MACROECONOMIC BACKGROUND, 1987–94

Looking first at overall economic growth as measured in the
national accounts, Table 4.1 shows that the period between 1987
and 1994 was one of fluctuating fortunes from year to year but
overall the experience was of substantial growth. After the
stagnation of the early and mid-1980s, 1987–90 saw an accelerat-
ing recovery, with both GNP and GDP growth reaching a
remarkable 7 per cent in real terms in 1990. The re-emergence of
global recession brought this expansion to an abrupt end, and
1991–93 saw very much lower growth rates of 1-3 per cent. In
1994, however, growth surged and reached about 7 per cent once
again. Between 1987 and 1994, then, overall growth in real GNP
amounted to about 33 per cent, and for GDP the corresponding
figure was 37 per cent. (By contrast the 1980–87 period, the focus
of our earlier work comparing poverty in the 1987 ESRI household survey and the 1980 HBS, saw real GDP growth of only 16
per cent.) The population fell during the late 1980s but this was
reversed in the early 1990s so that by 1994 it was little different
to 1987. Thus, as the table also shows, growth in real GNP per
head was faster than overall growth in the first part of the period
and slower in the second half, but taking 1987–94 as a whole real
GNP per head rose at about the same rate as real GNP. The
annual rate of price inflation, whether measured by the CPI or by

GNP or GDP deflators, was relatively low throughout, with prices increasing by about 20 per cent overall from 1987 to 1994. GNP in nominal terms had thus risen by about 63 per cent over the period.

TABLE 4.1: ANNUAL CHANGE IN REAL GROSS NATIONAL PRODUCT, GROSS DOMESTIC PRODUCT, AND GNP PER HEAD AND IN CONSUMER PRICES, 1987–94

Year	GNP*	GDP*	GNP per Head*	CPI
	% Change in Constant Prices			% Change
1988	2.5	4.5	3.0	2.1
1989	5.4	6.3	6.0	4.0
1990	7.3	7.1	7.4	3.4
1991	1.9	1.3	1.4	3.2
1992	2.0	3.6	1.4	3.0
1993	3.0	3.0	2.6	1.5
1994	7.4	6.6	7.1	2.4
1987–94	33.4	37.0	32.5	21.3

* Based on average of income and output constant price series.
Source: NIE 1994, 1995 Tables A, B.

In terms of household living standards and poverty, with which the present study is concerned, it is income accruing to house-holds which is of greatest interest. Table 4.2 shows the overall increase from 1987–94 in nominal and real terms in aggregate income going to "households and private non-profit institutions", the nearest one can get in the Irish national accounts to a total for private households, and in its components. Remuneration of employees, including social security contributions made by employers and before deduction of income tax or employees' PRSI contributions, increased by 60 per cent in nominal terms. Income from agriculture rose less rapidly, but income from other self-employment almost doubled in nominal terms. Interest, dividends and rent is estimated to have risen by about 37 per cent (a precise figure is not available because recent methodological revisions in the national accounts affecting this item have not been carried through back to 1987).[1] Transfers to households, mostly compris-

---

[1] In the 1995 national accounts the CSO significantly revised upwards the estimate for imputed rents, as part of the harmonisation of national accounts methodology across the EU. The revised series has so far been published only back to 1990, so here we have calculated the 1987-1990

ing social welfare payments, rose by 45 per cent. Overall, then, aggregate income going to "households and private non-profit institutions" rose by 56 per cent in nominal terms. With taxes on income and wealth rising by almost the same percentage, personal disposable income also rose by 56 per cent between 1987 and 1994. Deflating by the increase in prices over the period, we see that aggregate income before and after income tax and social security contributions were each 29 per cent higher in real terms in 1994 than they had been in 1987. Since these are income aggregates, changes in the number of persons and households over which they are spread will also affect living standards. As already noted, between 1987 and 1994 the population increased marginally (by less than 1 per cent), so the rise in personal disposable income per head is only slightly below that in the aggregate. However, the number of private households is estimated to have increased by about 10 per cent. This means that personal disposable income averaged over households increased less rapidly than the overall aggregate, by about 42 per cent in nominal terms and 18 per cent in real terms over the period. Of course, in assessing the implications for household living standards one would then take into account the decline in average household size that has taken place, from about 3.4 to 3.1 persons per household.[2]

Other sources of data on trends in incomes are also worth mentioning. The CSO's Quarterly Industrial Inquiry shows the index of average gross earnings for all employees (industrial, clerical or managerial) in industry increasing by about 44 per cent between 1987 and 1994. For industrial workers only, the increase was less: the actual earnings figures are published and were £198 per week in 1987 and £265 in 1994, a rise of 34 per cent. After deducting income tax, PRSI contributions and income levies, average net earnings of industrial workers will then have risen by 40-43 per cent (depending on whether a single person's or married couple's tax allowances are available). The direct tax burden at this particular income level thus fell considerably over the period, but the impact of changes in income tax and PRSI contributions structures will vary with the income level involved.

---

change on the old basis and the 1990-1994 one on the new basis, and then combined the two.

[2] This average is based on the number of persons in private households.

TABLE 4.2: CHANGE IN PERSONAL INCOME AND ITS COMPONENTS, 1987–94

	Current Prices	*Constant Prices***
	%	%
Remuneration of employees (including employers' social insurance contributions)	60.0	33.0
Income of independent traders		
— Agriculture	43.2	19.0
— Non-agriculture	95.1	62.2
Interest, dividends and rent	37.0*	13.9*
Current transfers	44.6	20.2
Personal income of households and private non-profit institutions	56.0*	29.7*
Taxes on personal income and wealth	57.2	30.7
Personal disposable income	55.7*	29.4*
Personal disposable income per head	54.6*	28.5*
Personal disposable income per household	42.0*	18.0*

* Estimated, because of discontinuity in NIE with increase in imputed rent from 1990 only.
** Deflated by GNP deflator based on average of income and output constant price series.
Source: NIE 1994, 1995 Tables B, 12 and 13.

Against this background of substantial growth in real incomes, what was happening in the labour market? Table 4.3 shows that total numbers in employment took some time to respond to the pick-up in economic growth, but then rose dramatically in 1990. Employment then mirrored growth, with little growth to 1993 but then a sharp increase in 1994. This meant that by 1994 there had been a very considerable increase, of 92,000, in the numbers at work compared with 1987. However labour force growth was also very rapid, amounting to 77,000 over the period, with the result that the numbers unemployed fell by only 15,000. (These figures are from the annual Labour Force Survey, and unemployment is measured on the basis of respondents' descriptions of their principal economic status, not whether they are on the Live Register; they are not therefore affected by the results of the recent CSO study of the labour force status of those signing on the Register). An important factor contributing to the increase in the labour force was that net emigration, although it was high in 1988-89, almost ceased from 1990. The unemployment rate of 17.6 per cent in 1987 was thus down only to 15.6 per cent by 1994, despite the impressive jobs growth.

TABLE 4.3: LABOUR MARKET DEVELOPMENTS, 1987–94

Year	At Work	Unemployed	Labour Force	Unemployment Rate	Migration
			('000)		
1987	1,090	233	1,323	17.6	-23
1988	1,090	218	1,308	16.7	-42
1989	1,088	201	1,289	15.6	-44
1990	1,134	176	1,310	13.4	-23
1991	1,134	208	1,342	15.5	-2
1992	1,139	221	1,360	16.3	2
1993	1,146	230	1,376	16.7	-6
1994	1,182	218	1,400	15.6	-10

Source: Labour Force Survey.

As well as the numbers unemployed, the duration of unemployment being experienced is also important. In 1987 about 64 per cent of the unemployed had been in that position for at least a year — the conventional definition of long-term unemployment. By 1994 this had fallen slightly, to 61 per cent. The fall was more pronounced for men than women: in 1987 68 per cent of male unemployed were long-term unemployed and by 1994 this was down to 65 per cent, whereas for women the corresponding figures were 55 per cent and 54 per cent.[3] This decline was partly attributable to a substantial increase in the numbers on state direct employment schemes aimed primarily at the long-term unemployed; by 1994, a total of 34,500 people were participating in such schemes, compared with about 10,000 in 1987.

The final aspect of changes between 1987 and 1994 to be sketched in at this stage is the one which is crucial to the position of those relying on state transfers, namely, what happened to

---

[3] These figures on unemployment duration are from special tabulations from the Labour Force Surveys, using the ILO definition of unemployment taking reported job search activity into account rather than that based on principal economic status (see Sexton and O'Connell, 1996, Table 3.5). They are distinct from data on length of time signing on the Live Register.

social welfare rates over the period. Table 4.4 shows the rates payable for single adults and for couples by scheme in each of these years (from July). We see that the increase in the basic personal rate between 1987 and 1994 varied a great deal across schemes, ranging from 29 per cent for both the contributory and non-contributory Old Age Pensions up to 73 per cent for Supplementary Welfare Allowance (SWA) and short-term Unemployment Assistance (UA). The increases for schemes for widows/widowers, lone parents and those on Invalidity Pension were towards the bottom of the range, at about 30-32 per cent, while the personal rate for Unemployment and Disability Benefits rose by an intermediate 44 per cent. Long-term Unemployment Assistance rose by over 60 per cent. This pattern reflects the strategy adopted over the period, in line with the recommendations of the Commission on Social Welfare (1986), to concentrate on bringing up what were the lowest rates. By 1994 there had therefore been a good deal of convergence in the rates paid across the different schemes: the lowest basic personal rate in 1994 (for SWA) was 83 per cent of the highest one (contributory Old Age Pension), whereas in 1987 the corresponding figure was 62 per cent.

Implementing this strategy involved increasing UA and SWA substantially in real terms. The Consumer Price Index rose by 21 per cent between 1987 and 1994, which means that the real value of UA and SWA increased by between 33 and 43 per cent over that period. At the other end of the scale, Old Age and Survivor's pensions rose by only 6-7 per cent in real terms. Unemployment and Disability Benefit rose by about 19 per cent in real terms.

As well as taking the change in prices as a point of comparison, the change in social welfare payments relative to other incomes is also highly relevant. This will be examined in detail below using the data on incomes in our 1987 and 1994 surveys, but it is worth noting at this stage that SWA and UA also rose much faster than average industrial earnings. As mentioned earlier, average industrial earnings in the QII increased in nominal terms by 34 per cent before tax and about 40 per cent after tax over this period, whereas SWA and UA rose by over 60 per cent. Flat-rate Unemployment Benefit rose by about the same as average after-tax earnings, but the additional Pay-Related Benefit was being phased out over this period so a substantial proportion of recipients saw a smaller percentage increase. Growth in Old Age and Survivor's pensions lagged significantly behind average earnings.

TABLE 4.4: SOCIAL WELFARE RATES, 1987 AND 1994 (FROM JULY)

Scheme	Personal Rate			With Adult Dependant*		
	1987	1994		1987	1994	
	£ per week		% increase	£ per week		% increase
Contributory Old Age Pension (under 80)**	55.10	71.00	28.9	90.20	116.20	28.8
Survivor's (Widow's/ Widower's) Contributory Pension, Deserted Wife's Benefit (under 66)**	49.50	64.50	30.30	—	—	—
UB/DB	42.30	61.00	44.2	69.70	97.60	40.0
Invalidity Pension (under 65)**	48.50	62.60	29.1	80.00	103.90	29.9
Non-contributory OAP (under 80) **	47.10	61.00	29.5	94.20	122.00	29.5
Widow's/Deserted Wives/Prisoner's Wives Non-contributory Pension (under 66)**	46.20	61.00	32.0	—	—	—
UA short-term***	34.00/ 35.10	58.90	73.2/ 67.8	58.70/ 60.40	95.50	62.7/ 58.1
UA long-term	37.80/ 36.60	61.00	61.4/ 66.7	65.00/ 63.20	97.60	50.2/ 54.4
Supplementary Welfare Allowance	34.00	58.90	73.2	58.70	95.50	62.7
Lone Parent's (Unmarried Mother's) Allowance, with 1 child	57.80	76.20	31.8	—	—	—
Disabled Person's Maintenance Allowance	44.50	61.00	37.1	69.80	97.60	39.8

* Dependant aged under 66 unless otherwise stated.

** These basic rates do not include the Living Alone Allowance payable to those aged 66 or over and living alone; a higher rate than shown is paid for those aged over 80.

*** In 1987, the lower rates shown applied to rural and the higher rates to urban areas; by 1994 this distinction had been abolished.

As well as the personal rate, Table 4.4 also shows the change in the rate paid by the various social welfare schemes for a couple between 1987 and 1994. This shows that for UA, UB/DB and SWA the percentage increase for a couple was lower than that for a single adult. This means that the equivalence scale implicit in these schemes changed over the period. In 1987 a couple received 1.65 times the basic adult payment in the case of UB, and the figure was as high as 1.72 for UA. By 1994 this ratio had fallen to 1.6 for UB and 1.62 for UA and SWA. This reflected the Commission on Social Welfare's recommendation that the appropriate ratio was 1.6. (As discussed in Callan, Nolan and Whelan, 1996, this recommendation was not however based on an in-depth empirical examination of the issue by the Commission or on Irish evidence). Particularly for UA and SWA, then, the increase for a couple was about 10 percentage points less than that for a single adult over the period — still a substantial rise in real terms and ahead of average industrial earnings. For old age pensions, on the other hand, the percentage increase for a couple was the same as that for a single adult (in the case of the non-contributory pension, because both spouses receive the full personal rate).

As far as child income support is concerned, in 1987 the Child Dependant Additions (CDAs) paid to social welfare recipients varied considerably across schemes and family sizes. Focusing only on UB, UA and SWA, for example, the rate per child ranged from £8.40 to £10.80 depending on which of the schemes was involved and whether it was the first, second etc. (dependent) child in the family. Child Benefit, paid for all dependent children irrespective of the parents' social welfare status, amounted to £15.05 per month (with a higher amount for sixth and subsequent children in a family). For the purpose of illustration, the average CDA across these schemes and across children 1-4 in a family in 1987 was £8.88, and adding on Child Benefit brings the total support for those in receipt of these schemes to £12.38 per child per week. By 1994, CDAs had been greatly simplified and harmonised within and across schemes, as had been recommended by the Commission on Social Welfare. UB, UA and SWA each now paid £13.20 for each child, irrespective of family size. Child Benefit had been increased to £20.00 for each of the first three children and £23.00 for fourth and subsequent children. The total support per child for those depending on these schemes, again averaging across children 1-4, therefore amounted to £18.02 by 1994. This represents an increase of 46 per cent since 1987.

Since the personal rate for UA and SWA rose by significantly
more than that, this means that the equivalence scale implicit in
these schemes has also changed as far as children are concerned.
In 1987, the additional amount paid for a child was about 1.32 for
long-term UA and 1.35 for short-term UA and SWA. By 1994, the
corresponding figures were 1.30 and 1.31. (For UB there was a
marginal fall from 1.31 to 1.30).

4.3 METHODOLOGICAL ASPECTS OF INCOME POVERTY LINES

In this section we discuss the methodological issues which arise
in constructing relative income poverty lines, on which much of
our analysis relies. We also discuss how income lines held
constant in real terms from a base year can be derived in a way
which helps to provide a rounded picture of the changes in income
poverty over time.

There are four main steps in defining a relative income poverty
line. First, one must define the *unit of analysis*. Second, one must
specify an *equivalence scale* in order to adjust incomes with
respect to differences in the needs of the chosen unit — for
example, households of different size and composition. Third, a
method of averaging equivalent incomes must be chosen. Fourth,
one must specify the *proportions of average income* which are to
be used as a poverty line cut-off. We deal with each of these issues
in turn.

As noted in Chapter 2, the household is the commonest *unit of
analysis* in studies of poverty. Implicitly, analysis at household
level treats all members of the household as if they had the same
standard of living. There may, however, be differences in living
standards between family units comprising say, parents and their
dependent children, and older children living as adults in the
family home. Within family units, there may also be differences in
living standards between individual members, for example,
between spouses. Analysis at sub-household unit level has been
undertaken using the 1987 ESRI data by Callan (1994), Cantillon
(1994) and Cantillon and Nolan (1996); and a detailed study of
the distribution of resources within families was undertaken by
Rottman (1994), using data drawn mainly from the 1989 follow-up
survey, which contained more detailed questions on the internal
allocation of resources within families. These investigations give a
much more detailed picture of sub-household and intra-family

issues than most international studies of poverty. In this first report using 1994 data, results are only available at household level; some sub-household level analysis will be possible at a later stage.

A detailed discussion of the issues involved in selecting *equivalence scales* is contained in Callan, Nolan et al. (1989, Chapter 5). Three scales were used in that study, which taken together, cover a broad range of possible scales, encompassing most of those used in previous research on poverty and income distribution in Ireland. In order to produce comparable results, we use the same three scales here, as set out in Table 4.5.[4] In order to allow comparisons with results from the Household Budget Surveys of 1973 and 1980, children are defined as those aged under 14 years of age.

TABLE 4.5: EQUIVALENCE SCALES USED IN THE ANALYSIS

	Equivalence Scale		
	A	*B*	*C*
	(SWA 1987)	*(UK scale)*	*(EU scale)*
First adult in household	1.00	1.00	1.00
Other adults (aged 14-64)	0.66	0.60	0.70
Children (aged under 14)	0.33	0.40	0.50

The derivation of these scales:
Scale A approximates the scales implicit in Irish social welfare rates in 1987.
Scale B is widely used in the UK.
Scale C has been widely used in the analysis of poverty at EU level, by Eurostat and others.

The background to the chosen scales can be set out briefly as follows. Equivalence scale A approximates the relationships implicit in major Irish social welfare schemes (Unemployment Benefit and Assistance and Supplementary Welfare Allowance) as they operated in 1987. The scale implicit in these schemes by 1994 is somewhat different, as described in the previous section, with lower weights for additional adults and children. However, it

---

[4] Note that although the set of scales are the same as employed in our earlier studies such as Callan, Nolan et al. (1989), the labels A and C have now been reversed because we tend to pay most attention to the 1/0.66/0.33 scale and it is therefore more helpful to refer to it as Scale A.

is informative to use an unchanged equivalence scale across time, and this one provides a useful benchmark which is still close to the relativities implicit in the social welfare system itself. Equivalence scale B has been widely used in the analysis of poverty and income distribution in the UK. It is similar to scales derived from the UK Supplementary Benefit scheme in the 1980s. It incorporates a slightly lower weighting for the needs of additional adults than scale A (which is in fact identical with that implicit in most Irish social welfare schemes by 1994) and a higher weighting for the needs of children (between 25 and 30 per cent higher than that in most Irish social welfare schemes in 1994). Equivalence scale C is a scale which has been widely used in the analysis of poverty at EU level. (Scales which further differentiate between children of different ages were also tested in earlier research based on the 1987 survey including Nolan and Farrell (1990), and shown there not to affect the overall extent of measured income poverty: this is none the less an issue which will be revisited with the 1994 survey data in future work.)

The third issue to be resolved is the *method of arriving at an average income figure* from which the poverty lines are derived. As discussed in Chapter 2, the mean can be seen as preferable in being easily understood, but if the mean is highly sensitive to a small number of very high incomes, statistics based on the median may be preferred. In the present context, we use mean income as the basis for most of the measures of relative income poverty; but also examine trends with median income-based poverty lines, to examine the possible sensitivity of the results. A further choice arises in that mean income per equivalent adult can be averaged over households, or averaged over all individuals (adults and children) to provide a figure for the "representative person" rather than the "representative household". Since our ultimate interest is in the number of persons in poverty, there is a strong case to be made for averaging equivalent income over persons. This is the procedure adopted in the UK's official statistics on Households Below Average Income (HBAI) as discussed in Chapter 2. However, a case can also be made for using the income of the representative household, and figures based on incomes averaged over households are in any case required for comparisons with our earlier published results. In this chapter, we therefore show results for both approaches.

The final element of the methodology is the selection of pro-portions of average income which serve as *cut-offs to define the poverty line income.* The most common procedure is to use 50 per cent of mean or median income. But a key point from the international literature, and confirmed by our own work on poverty measurement in Ireland, is the need to use a number of income cut-offs in order to test the sensitivity of conclusions to the precise location of the poverty line. For this reason we conduct much of our analysis using relative income poverty lines at 40, 50 and 60 per cent of mean income per adult equivalent. We also examine the sensitivity of trends in the 1987–94 period to the use of cut-offs at 50, 60 and 70 per cent of median income.

Finally, we have already discussed the need to complement results based on relative income poverty lines with an examination of changes in real incomes and in the numbers falling below income lines held constant in real terms over time. The discussion in Chapter 2 will have made clear our belief that the search for an "absolute" poverty line which would have relevance in a developed country such as Ireland is a fruitless one. In monitoring changes over a period such as 1987–94, the most satisfactory procedure to deriving income lines held constant in real terms appears to be to take relative income lines for the base year and simply index these to prices over time. In that way, the comparison between 1987 and 1994 using relative income lines for each year can be complemented by a comparison using a range of lines which represent the same purchasing power in each year.

4.4 AGGREGATE RESULTS USING INCOME POVERTY LINES, 1994

The income concept employed throughout our analysis is disposable household income, as described in Chapter 3. Mean disposable income averaged over households in the 1994 Living in Ireland Survey was £280. This represents an increase of 42 per cent on the mean in the 1987 ESRI survey, which seems broadly consistent with the growth in incomes over the period indicated by other sources as described in Section 4.2.[5] Adjusting for household size and composition using the 3 alternative equivalence scales set out earlier and averaging over households produces the figures for average equivalent household income set

---

[5] As pointed out there, a direct comparison between income figures derived from the National Accounts and those in a household survey is not possible because of differences in definition and methods.

out in Table 4.6. Mean equivalent disposable household income
has risen since 1987 by about 50 per cent for each of the equivalence scales, more rapidly than mean unadjusted household
income because average household size has continued to fall.

TABLE 4.6: AVERAGE WEEKLY HOUSEHOLD EQUIVALENT INCOME
AND RELATIVE INCOME POVERTY LINES, LIVING IN IRELAND
SURVEY, 1994

	Equivalence Scale*		
	A	B	C
Income per adult equivalent averaged over households	£128.94	£130.90	£121.36
40% income poverty line for a single adult derived from this average	£51.58	£52.36	£48.54
50% income poverty line for a single adult derived from this average	£64.47	£65.45	£60.68
60% income poverty line for a single adult derived from this average	£77.36	£78.54	£72.82

* Equivalence scales defined in Table 4.5.

The table also shows the levels of the relative income poverty
lines implied by these means. We see that the 50 per cent relative
income poverty line based on equivalent income averaged over
households varies between £60.68 and £65.45 for a single person
household, depending on the equivalence scale used. These
income levels are close to those paid by many social welfare
schemes at the time of the Living in Ireland survey. As we saw in
the previous section, the basic personal rate for many schemes,
including Unemployment and Disability Benefits, long-term UA,
non-contributory Widow(er)'s and Old Age Pensions, and Disabled
Person's Maintenance Allowance was £61.00 per week from mid-
1994. The lowest rate, for short-term UA and SWA, was £58.90.
The 40 per cent relative income line for a single adult is in the
range £49-52, well below those social welfare rates, but is included
to facilitate comprehensive comparisons over time and across
countries. The 60 per cent relative income line for a single adult,
on the other hand, lies in the range £73-79 per week, which is well
above most of the social welfare rates prevailing at the time.

Table 4.7 shows the percentage of households and persons below these relative income poverty lines in 1994. We see that the percentage of persons falling below the 40 per cent line ranges from 7 to almost 11 per cent depending on the equivalence scale. The percentage in households below the 50 per cent line ranges from 21 to 23 per cent, while 34-35 per cent are below the 60 per cent income line. The sensitivity of the figures to the line and equivalence scale chosen highlights the need to explore trends in poverty and the composition of poor households using a number of cut-offs and equivalence scales. It also lends points to the importance of measures of poverty which go beyond simply "counting heads" and take into account, for those below an income poverty line, the gap between their incomes and the poverty line cut-off — which we employ in Section 4.5.

TABLE 4.7: PERCENTAGE BELOW ALTERNATIVE RELATIVE INCOME POVERTY LINES IN 1994

	Equivalence Scale*		
	A	*B*	*C*
Equivalent Income Averaged Over Households	*Percentage of Households / Persons Below Line*		
40 per cent poverty line:			
Percentage of households	5.0	5.3	7.0
Percentage of persons	6.8	7.6	10.7
50 per cent poverty line:			
Percentage of households	18.5	19.5	16.9
Percentage of persons	20.7	21.6	22.7
60 per cent poverty line:			
Percentage of households	34.6	34.4	33.3
Percentage of persons	34.0	33.9	35.2

* Equivalence scales defined in Table 4.5.

One common feature across the equivalence scales is that the proportion of persons below the income cut-offs is higher than the corresponding proportion of households. This indicates that households below the income cut-offs are somewhat larger than average. There has been a slight fall in the gap between the household size of "poor" households defined in this way, and that of other households, between 1987 and 1994. Household size has declined from about 3.6 to 3.3 in the general population, while the average for those below the 50 per cent line (under equivalence scale A) has fallen from about 4.2 persons to 3.6 persons per household.

The results presented so far have been based on equivalent income averaged over households, the procedure for constructing relative income lines adopted in Callan, Nolan et al. (1989) and subsequent work using the 1987 survey. As noted earlier, an alternative is to average equivalent income over individuals, as is the practice in the UK's Households Below Average Income, and it is of interest to assess how much difference this makes to the numbers below relative income lines. Average equivalent income over individuals with the different equivalence scales turns out to be between £5.00 and £7.00 per week lower than the averages for households: this reflects the fact that larger households are somewhat more likely to have low incomes per adult equivalent. Table 4.8 shows the percentage of persons below relative income lines using equivalent income averaged over individuals as benchmark. The lower poverty lines mean that poverty rates with the 50 per cent line are about 2-3 percentage points lower than in Table 4.7, and with the 60 per cent line they are 3-5 percentage points lower. The method of averaging does clearly matter, then, and it is important to ensure consistency in making comparisons over time or across countries. While flagging this as an issue for further attention, we revert in the remainder of this study to the benchmarks based on averaging across households, since that is the basis on which we can make comparisons with earlier years.

TABLE 4.8: RELATIVE POVERTY LINES BASED ON INCOME AVERAGED ACROSS INDIVIDUALS, 1994

	Equivalence Scale*		
Equivalent income averaged over persons	A	B	C
Percentage of persons below:			
40 per cent poverty line	5.3	5.7	7.1
50 per cent poverty line	18.2	19.7	19.1
60 per cent poverty line	31.4	31.3	30.3

* Equivalence scales defined in Table 4.5.

Before going on to consider how the results for 1994 compare with earlier years, it is necessary to consider the possible implications for these estimates of income poverty of the recent CSO study (CSO, 1996) on unemployment in the Labour Force Survey and the Live Register, mentioned in Chapter 3. This study suggested that some of those on the Live Register report themselves as in full- or part-time employment to the Labour Force Survey. While a small proportion of respondents to the Living in Ireland Survey are found to be "working and claiming", most of these are covered by the rules on systematic short-time work. This suggests that the phenomenon of "working and claiming" may be under-represented in the Living in Ireland Survey. If this is the case, it may arise for a number of different reasons (which are not mutually exclusive). First, those who are "working and claiming" in ways which are not covered by the rules of the social welfare system may be under-represented in the survey because of a higher non-response rate than for other groups. Second, respondents in this category may have misrepresented their situation in one of two ways: they may have reported their employment, but not their benefit receipt, or vice versa. (The under-representation of Live Register recipients in the Labour Force Survey, noted by Murphy and Walsh (1996), suggests that in that survey there may have been some tendency for individuals to report their employment but not their benefit receipt).

We have undertaken some initial work to examine the sensitivity of the estimates of aggregate poverty to the possible extent of "working and claiming", and to alternative explanations for its possible under-representation in the Living in Ireland survey. This work is in an exploratory phase, but some of the early results are of interest. The general approach has been to assign the status of "working and claiming" randomly to a subset of those reporting themselves as in employment, at weekly wage rates between £50.00 and £250.00; and/or to a subset of those reporting themselves as in receipt of Unemployment Benefit or Unemployment Assistance.[6] For those who are reported as in employment, and are assigned the "working and claiming" status, the amount of unemployment compensation is crudely assigned depending only on family composition and the earnings of a spouse. Those who are in receipt of benefit, and are assigned the "working and

---

[6] This approach helps in examining the possible sensitivity of results to either form of "misreporting" by respondents; but can also indicate sensitivity to possible differential non-response by those who are "working and claiming".

claiming" status, have an equal probability of being assigned a job with net income of £80.00, £110.00, £140.00, £170.00 or £200.00.

The CSO study indicated that 11 per cent of those on the Live Register who were interviewed in the Labour Force Survey reported themselves as in full-time employment; with a further 10 per cent in part-time employment. Given the difficulties in tracing individuals on the register (with some unknown or not resident at the address given), the total incidence of "working and claiming" could be somewhat higher than these figures. For exploratory purposes, therefore, we consider situations in which 10 per cent, 20 per cent or 30 per cent of the Live Register are in the "working and claiming" status. We consider situations in which all of those assigned to "working and claiming" status are initially in employment; all are initially unemployed and in receipt of benefit; or half are initially in employment and half unemployed.

The impact of these sensitivity tests on the aggregate incidence of relative income poverty is quite limited. Typically, the impact is to reduce the poverty rate by less than one percentage point. Even on the most extreme assumptions (30 per cent of the Live Register assumed to be "working and claiming", and all of this assigned to individuals initially unemployed), the impact is just over 1.5 percentage points at the highest poverty line (where the initial estimate is that almost 35 per cent of households fell below the 60 per cent relative income line). In part, this reflects the fact that the relative poverty line itself shifts up as mean income rises when account is taken of the additional incomes involved. But even if the poverty line is held fixed in money terms, the maximum reduction in poverty shown by the most extreme assumptions is about 2.5 percentage points (from the same 35 per cent level).

4.5 TRENDS IN INCOME POVERTY, 1987–94

We now proceed to the analysis of changes in income poverty between 1987, which up until now was the latest year for which data was available, and 1994. Table 4.9 presents the percentages of households and individuals falling below the 40, 50 and 60 per cent relative income poverty lines for 1987 and 1994.[7] With the 40

---

[7] Note that some revisions to the poverty rates for 1987 in Callan, Nolan et al., (1989) were published in Nolan and Callan (eds.) (1994). These related mainly to a small number of low incomes, which have some impact on head

per cent line, the new data for 1994 show a consistent fall since 1987 in the percentage of households below the line, while the percentage of persons below the line falls with scales B and C and remains unchanged with scale A. For the 50 per cent line, the percentage of households falling below the line rises with scales A and B but not C, and there is an increase in the percentage of persons falling below the line with all three equivalence scales. The size of the increase in the number of persons below the line is 1-2 percentage points depending on the scale employed. The 1994 data show a marked increase in the percentage of both households and persons below the 60 per cent line since 1987. For persons, there was a rise of 3-4 percentage points, and for households the increase was even greater.

TABLE 4.9: PERCENTAGE OF PERSONS BELOW RELATIVE INCOME POVERTY LINES, 1987 AND 1994

	*Equivalence Scale**					
	A		*B*		*C*	
	1987	*1994*	*1987*	*1994*	*1987*	*1994*
Percentage of Households Below Line:						
40 per cent line	6.2	5.0	7.6	5.3	8.9	7.0
50 per cent line	16.3	18.5	17.1	19.5	17.6	16.9
60 per cent line	28.5	34.6	29.1	34.4	27.7	33.3
Percentage of Persons Below Line:						
40 per cent line	6.8	6.8	9.3	7.6	11.8	10.7
50 per cent line	18.9	20.7	20.1	21.6	21.8	22.7
60 per cent line	29.8	34.0	31.0	33.9	32.2	35.2

* Equivalence scales defined in Table 4.5.

We have already stressed that head count measures of the percentage falling below a given poverty line have major limitations as summary measures of poverty. As discussed in

---

counts of poverty, and a greater impact on measures which take into account the depth and distribution of poverty gaps.

Chapter 2, more sophisticated measures are available, which take into account not only the extent of poverty as measured by a head count, but also the depth of income poverty and the distribution of income among the poor. Rather than simply concentrating on whether someone is below the income poverty line, this involves focusing on the gap between their income and the poverty line, their "poverty gap". Here we thus employ two summary measures based on this gap, drawing on Foster et al. (1984). The first is the per capita income gap (which we label P_2), the mean over all persons of the shortfalls below the income line.[8] This in effect combines information on the proportion of the sample falling below the poverty line and the depth of their poverty on average. Results for this measure for 1987 and 1994 with the 40 per cent, 50 per cent and 60 per cent lines, and for all three equivalence scales, are shown in Table 4.10. We see that, compared with 1987, the new data for 1994 show a fall in P_2 with the 40 and 50 per cent relative lines and little change with the 60 per cent line.

TABLE 4.10: PER PERSON INCOME GAPS (P_2) USING RELATIVE POVERTY LINES AND DIFFERENT EQUIVALENCE SCALES, 1987 AND 1994

*Equivalence Scale**	*Relative Poverty Line*					
	40%		*50%*		*60%*	
	1987	*1994*	*1987*	*1994*	*1987*	*1994*
A	0.020	0.010	0.044	0.034	0.077	0.075
B	0.024	0.011	0.049	0.039	0.083	0.079
C	0.027	0.015	0.056	0.046	0.091	0.087

* Equivalence scales defined in Table 4.5.

As well as the size of poverty gaps on average, we might however also care about how the poverty gaps are themselves distributed among those below the line, being most concerned by the existence of very large income gaps. The second measure of poverty discussed by Foster et al. (which we label P_3) is sensitive not only to the depth of poverty but also to its distribution. It involves squaring the proportionate income gaps and taking the mean of that variable, which has the effect of giving most weight

---

[8] Similar measures can be defined at household level, but in this exposition we concentrated on the application of the measures at person level.

to those whose income gaps are greatest, i.e., those with the lowest incomes. For P_3, there is a fall in the index between 1987 and 1994 with all the relative income lines and equivalence scales: even where the numbers below relative lines have risen, the fall in poverty gaps, especially in the highest poverty gaps, has been enough to bring about a decline in this depth and distribution sensitive measure.

TABLE 4.11: DISTRIBUTION-SENSITIVE POVERTY MEASURE (P_3) USING RELATIVE POVERTY LINES AND DIFFERENT EQUIVALENCE SCALES, 1987 AND 1994

Equivalence Scale*	Relative Poverty Line					
	40%		50%		60%	
	1987	1994	1987	1994	1987	1994
A	0.013	0.003	0.020	0.010	0.032	0.023
B	0.013	0.004	0.022	0.011	0.035	0.026
C	0.014	0.004	0.024	0.014	0.039	0.030

* Equivalence scales defined in Table 4.5.

The relative poverty lines used so far in comparing 1987 and 1994 are based on proportions of average equivalent household income. We have adverted on a number of occasions to the possible sensitivity of mean-based estimates to a small number of very high incomes reported at the top of the distribution. In order to guard against possible distortions arising from the sensitivity of the mean to outlying observations, we have also examined trends based on median incomes, which are not affected by outliers in the same way.[9] Median income per adult equivalent (under scale A) in 1987 was £68.50 per week, as against a mean income of £85.40. In 1994, the corresponding figures were £99.30 and £129.10 — an increase of 45 per cent in the median income per adult equivalent as against 51 per cent in the mean. Setting relative poverty lines at 50, 60 and 70 per cent of median income, in 1987 approximately 7 per cent, 17 per cent and 25 per cent of persons were below these lines. In 1994, however, these median-based cut-offs show

---

[9] If all households are ranked from poorest to richest, the median income is the income of the household ranked exactly half-way in the distribution: an equal number of households are found above it and below it in the income distribution.

the risk of poverty as 5 per cent, 15 per cent, and 26 per cent respectively. Using the median one thus only sees a rise in the percentage of persons in poverty between 1987 and 1994 with the highest poverty line, whereas, as we have seen, the mean-based lines showed an increase with both the 50 and 60 per cent lines.

In our analysis of trends we have concentrated thus far on purely relative income poverty lines. In our view, this is essential for the assessment of poverty over any considerable period when general living standards are changing, since perceptions and expectations as to what is acceptable will also change. It is also important to know what has been happening to real incomes, however: for example, one would want to distinguish between a situation where the incomes of the poor are rising in real terms but lagging behind the average in the society and one where real incomes of the poor are falling while the average is stable. Although a poverty standard which is fixed in real income terms will lose relevance over a lengthy period of growth, in a relatively short time period such as the 1987 to 1994 one it is useful to look at how household incomes have evolved *vis-à-vis* such a standard. In particular, it is of interest to know how many persons now fall below real income standards corresponding in real terms to the relative income poverty line cut-offs for 1987. Table 4.12 presents such results.

The Consumer Price Index (CPI) and the National Accounts Personal Consumption deflator (PCD) both rose by approximately 21.5 per cent between 1987 and 1994 (whereas as we have seen mean household income rose by 42 per cent in nominal terms between the 1987 and 1994 surveys). Thus, the 1987 income standards uprated for price changes only to 1994 terms come to approximately £41, £52 and £62 respectively for the 40 per cent, 50 per cent and 60 per cent cut-offs (with equivalence scale A). As would be expected, during a period of significant real income growth, the proportions of persons falling below a given real income standard have fallen. The falls are particularly large under scales A and B, where the risk of poverty has fallen by more than two-thirds at the 40 per cent cut-off, more than half at the 50 per cent cut-off, and more than one-third at the 60 per cent line. The falls under scale C at the 50 and 60 per cent lines, although not so large, are still very substantial.

TABLE 4.12: PROPORTIONS OF PERSONS BELOW A COMMON REAL
INCOME STANDARD, 1987 AND 1994

Real Income Standard	Equivalence Scale*					
	A		B		C	
Percentage of Persons Below Line:						
	1987	*1994*	*1987*	*1994*	*1987*	*1994*
40 per cent line, 1987	6.8	1.8	9.3	1.8	11.8	2.3
50 per cent line, 1987	18.9	7.2	20.1	7.7	21.8	10.7
60 per cent line, 1987	29.8	18.4	31.0	19.8	32.2	20.3

* Equivalence scales defined in Table 4.5.

This forms a very important part of the backdrop against which
results based on relative income poverty lines must be evaluated.
It stands in marked contrast with the period 1980 to 1987, when
real household incomes changed very little on average and thus
the trends in the proportion of households below poverty lines
held constant in real terms were very similar to those based on
relative income lines. It must also be contrasted with the
situation in the UK, where — as discussed in Chapter 2 — figures
on both the proportions below relative income lines and lines held
fixed in real terms are regularly produced. The debate in the UK
has concentrated not only the rapid increase in numbers below
relative income lines, but also on whether those at the bottom of
the income distribution have seen real income increases of any
size during the 1980s and into the 1990s. In the Irish case, it is
clear that while the proportions below the higher relative lines
have risen between 1987 and 1994, this has been in the context of
quite substantial increases in real incomes throughout the
distribution.

To understand the factors underlying the observed changes in
income poverty between 1987 and 1994, it will be necessary to
look in detail at changes in the profile of households below the
income thresholds, which is the subject of the next chapter.
However, some key features may be mentioned at this stage. We
saw in Section 4.2 that employee income and income from self-
employment grew more rapidly than transfer income in aggregate
between 1987 and 1994. While support rates for the lowest-paying

social welfare schemes in 1987 rose by more than average net
earnings or household income between 1987 and 1994, other rates
rose by less. Incomes for many social welfare recipients have thus
risen by less than the relative income poverty lines. Despite the
fall in the unemployment rate, then, this has clearly been
sufficient to increase the percentage of persons falling below the
higher mean-based relative lines. However, the summary
measures taking the extent to which people actually fall below
these relative lines show a rather different picture, because
poverty gaps have fallen on average and particularly because the
numbers on very low incomes have fallen sharply. Farm incomes
in the 1987 survey (which measured farm incomes in 1986) were
particularly low, and the rapid increase in farm incomes by the
1994 survey was a major factor in the fall in numbers with zero or
very low incomes, as was the relatively rapid rise in income from
self-employment. The fact that the most substantial increases in
social welfare rates over the period were for the schemes which
paid least in 1987 also contributed to the decline in poverty gaps.
Analysing the changing risk and incidence of poverty for
households of different types and in different situations, as we do
in the next chapter, will help to identify the role of these and other
influences.

4.6 TRENDS IN INCOME POVERTY, 1973–94

We now look at trends in poverty over the longer period from
1973, rather than simply 1987 to 1994, to put recent developments in longer-term context. Our earlier work compared the
relative poverty line results from the 1987 survey with the
corresponding estimates which we derived from the 1973 and
1980 Household Budget Surveys carried out by the CSO. (Our
analysis of the micro-data from the budget surveys was kindly
facilitated by the CSO). We begin once again by focusing on the
percentage of households and persons below (mean-based)
relative income poverty lines.[10] Table 4.13 presents the proportions of households and individuals falling below the 50 per cent
relative income poverty line for the years 1973 and 1980 (using

---

[10] There have been some corrections to the estimates of poverty rates
previously published for 1973. Head count measures now show poverty
rates between half and one percentage point higher, while the
depth/distribution sensitive indices are slightly higher.

Household Budget Survey data), for 1987 (using ESRI Survey data) and for 1994 (using the Living in Ireland Survey data), for the three equivalence scales as before. Figure 4.1 illustrates the pattern for persons.

Over this time-span we see the proportion of households below the 50 per cent line fell between 1973 and 1987 for each equivalence scale, then rose to 1994 with scales A and B back to about the 1973 rate but continued to fall with scale C. The proportion of persons falling below that line rose slightly between 1973 and 1980, more rapidly between 1980 and 1987, and continued to rise to 1994 with all three equivalence scales. The relative poverty rates for persons in 1994 are considerably higher than in 1973 with all three scales.

TABLE 4.13: PERCENTAGE OF HOUSEHOLDS AND PERSONS BELOW 50 PER CENT RELATIVE INCOME POVERTY LINE, 1973–94

	Equivalence Scale			
	1973 *HBS*	*1980* *HBS*	*1987* *ESRI*	*1994* *LII*
Equivalence Scale*				
	Percentage of Households Below Line			
A	18.3	16.8	16.3	18.5
B	18.8	17.6	17.1	19.5
C	18.9	17.2	17.6	16.9
	Percentage of Persons Below Line			
A	15.5	16.2	18.9	20.7
B	16.8	17.4	20.1	21.6
C	18.6	19.2	21.8	22.7

* Equivalence scales defined in Table 4.5.

Table 4.14 presents corresponding results at the 40 per cent line, with the results for persons again shown in the figure. There is a general trend towards a lower proportion of households in poverty over the entire period 1973–94, but a rise in the relative size of low income households leads to a more complex pattern in terms of the proportion of persons. The proportion of persons falling below the line rose between 1973 and 1980, between 1980 and 1987 the trend depends on the equivalence scale chosen, and between 1987 and 1994 the percentage of persons below the line falls with scales B and C and remains unchanged with scale A.

Compared with 1973, the poverty rates for persons in 1994 are slightly lower with scales A and B but higher with scale C.

FIGURE 4.1: PROPORTION OF INDIVIDUALS IN HOUSEHOLDS BELOW RELATIVE POVERTY LINES, 1973–94

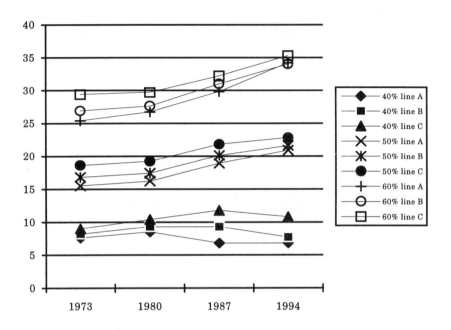

Table 4.15 shows the results at the 60 per cent relative income line. The proportion of households below the line rose slightly between 1973 and 1987 with scales A and B but fell with equivalence scale C, but then rose markedly between 1987 and 1994 with all three scales. The proportion of persons falling below this line, as illustrated in Figure 4.1, rose in all cases between 1973 and 1987 and then again between 1987 and 1994. As a result, the percentage of persons below the 60 per cent relative income line in 1994 was between 6-9 percentage points higher than it had been in 1973.

TABLE 4.14: PERCENTAGE OF HOUSEHOLDS AND PERSONS BELOW 40 PER CENT RELATIVE POVERTY LINE, 1973–94

	Equivalence Scale			
	1973 HBS	1980 HBS	1987 ESRI	1994 LII
Equivalence Scale*				
	Percentage of Households Below the Line			
A	9.1	8.0	6.2	5.0
B	9.3	8.6	7.6	5.3
C	8.5	8.5	8.9	7.0
	Percentage of Persons Below the Line			
A	7.6	8.5	6.8	6.8
B	8.2	9.3	9.3	7.6
C	9.0	10.4	11.8	10.7

* Equivalence scales defined in Table 4.5.

TABLE 4.15: PERCENTAGE OF HOUSEHOLDS AND PERSONS BELOW 60 PER CENT RELATIVE POVERTY LINE, 1973–94

	Equivalence Scale			
	1973 HBS	1980 HBS	1987 ESRI	1994 LII
Equivalence Scale*				
	Percentage of Households Below the Line			
A	27.3	27.6	28.5	34.6
B	27.9	27.9	29.1	34.4
C	28.8	27.9	27.7	33.3
	Percentage of Persons Below the Line			
A	25.4	26.7	29.8	34.0
B	26.9	27.6	31.0	33.9
C	29.4	29.7	32.2	35.2

* Equivalence scales defined in Table 4.5.

Once again, head-counts of the percentage of households below the income poverty lines have to be complemented by alternative summary poverty measures which take into account the depth of their income shortfalls. Results for the P_2 and P_3 measures described earlier for the four points in time are presented for the 40 per cent, 50 per cent and 60 per cent lines, and for all three equivalence scales, in Tables 4.16 and 4.17. The "depth sensitive" per capita income gap measure (P_2) shows a consistent rise at all poverty cut-offs and equivalence scales between 1973 and 1980. The pattern between 1980 and 1987 is that P_2 falls at the 40 per cent line, was approximately constant at the 50 per cent line, and increased slightly at the 60 per cent line. Between 1987 and 1994 P_2 fell with the 40 and 50 per cent relative lines and showed little change with the 60 per cent line. Over the entire period 1973–94, this measure fell with the 40 line, fell much less or not at all with the 50 per cent line, and rose with the 60 per cent line.

Table 4.17 and Figure 4.2 show that the "depth and distribution sensitive" measure, P_3, again falls consistently between 1973 and 1980 across all lines and scales. Between 1980 and 1987 it generally either fell or was stable, while it fell consistently between 1987 and 1994 with all the relative income lines and equivalence scales. By 1994, this measure of income poverty was below the 1973 values for all relative lines and equivalence scales. It has therefore fallen even where the numbers below relative lines have risen, as they have most markedly with the 60 per cent line: the fall in poverty gaps, especially in the highest poverty gaps, has been enough to outweigh the increase in numbers and bring about a decline in the depth and distribution sensitive measure.

TABLE 4.16: PER PERSON INCOME GAPS (P$_2$) USING RELATIVE POVERTY LINES AND DIFFERENT EQUIVALENCE SCALES, 1973–94

Equivalence Scale*	Relative Poverty Line											
	40%				50%				60%			
	1973	1980	1987	1994	1973	1980	1987	1994	1973	1980	1987	1994
A	0.020	0.027	0.020	0.010	0.039	0.046	0.044	0.034	0.066	0.074	0.077	0.075
B	0.022	0.029	0.024	0.011	0.042	0.049	0.049	0.039	0.071	0.078	0.083	0.079
C	0.024	0.031	0.027	0.015	0.046	0.054	0.056	0.046	0.078	0.085	0.091	0.087

* Equivalence scales defined in Table 4.5.

TABLE 4.17: DISTRIBUTION-SENSITIVE POVERTY MEASURE (P$_3$) USING RELATIVE POVERTY LINES AND DIFFERENT EQUIVALENCE SCALES, 1973–94

Equivalence Scale*	Relative Poverty Line											
	40%				50%				60%			
	1973	1980	1987	1994	1973	1980	1987	1994	1973	1980	1987	1994
A	0.010	0.016	0.013	0.003	0.017	0.023	0.020	0.010	0.028	0.034	0.032	0.023
B	0.010	0.016	0.013	0.004	0.018	0.024	0.022	0.011	0.030	0.036	0.035	0.026
C	0.011	0.018	0.014	0.004	0.020	0.019	0.024	0.014	0.033	0.040	0.039	0.030

* Equivalence scales defined in Table 4.5.

FIGURE 4.2: DEPTH- AND DISTRIBUTION-SENSITIVE POVERTY
MEASURE, 1973–94

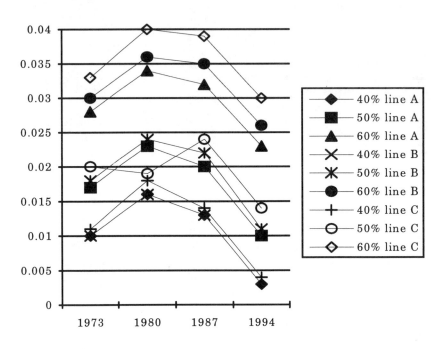

4.7 CONCLUSIONS

In this chapter, relative income poverty lines have been applied to
the data from the 1994 Living in Ireland Survey, and comparisons
made with the 1987 ESRI survey and the 1980 and 1973
Household Budget Surveys. We began with a review of the
macroeconomic background to the 1987–94 period, which
highlighted relatively rapid growth in GNP, an increase of about
20 per cent in real terms in personal disposable income per
household and in average net earnings in industry, and a fall in
the unemployment rate (as measured by the Labour Force
Survey) of about 2 percentage points.

As in our analysis of 1987, a range of relative income lines and
equivalence scales has been employed. Compared with 1987, the
main findings were that the percentage of persons below the 40
per cent relative line had fallen or was unchanged by 1994, but
the proportion below the 50 and even more so the 60 per cent line
had increased. The percentage of persons below the 60 per cent

line was 3-4 percentage points higher in 1994 than in 1987. However, distribution-sensitive summary poverty measures, taking into account not only numbers below the lines but how far their incomes are below the line, fell between 1987 and 1994 with all the income lines. The overall conclusion about the trend in relative income poverty between 1987 and 1994 is thus that the numbers affected were higher in 1994, but the depth of their income poverty was lower on average.

Poverty lines held fixed in real terms from 1987 were also applied to the 1994 data. Since there was significant real income growth over the period, by 1994 the numbers below these "absolute" thresholds were considerably lower than in 1987. This is an important part of the backdrop against which trends in relative income poverty should be assessed.

Over the longer period from 1973, the percentage of persons below the 50 and 60 per cent relative income poverty lines in 1994 was considerably higher than in 1973. Other summary measures show a rather different picture, with a measure taking the depth and distribution of poverty shortfalls into account being lower in 1994 than in 1973 for all relative lines and equivalence scales.

The implications for estimates of income poverty of the recent CSO study (CSO, 1996) on unemployment in the Labour Force Survey and the Live Register were considered. That study suggested that some of those on the Live Register report themselves as in full- or part-time employment to the Labour Force Survey. We have examined the sensitivity of the estimates of aggregate poverty to the possible extent of "working and claiming", and to alternative explanations for its possible under-representation in the Living in Ireland survey. The impact of these sensitivity tests on the aggregate incidence of relative income poverty was seen to be quite limited.

The change in social welfare support rates relative to other incomes is a key factor underlying the observed change in relative income poverty rates between 1987 and 1994. Although support rates for the lowest-paying social welfare schemes in 1987 had risen by more than average net earnings or household income by 1994, other rates had lagged behind, so the risk of being below the higher relative income lines rose for many of those relying on social welfare. However, the summary measures taking the extent to which people actually fall below these relative lines show a rather different picture, because they are significantly affected by the numbers with zero or very low incomes, most of whom are self-employed or farmers. The much better situation of farmers in the 1994 survey, compared with the particularly bad year covered by the 1987 survey, was an important factor in reducing the number of very low incomes. The relatively rapid increase in self-employment income and in what had been the lowest rates of social welfare support will also have contributed to the fall in the depth- and distribution-sensitive poverty measures between 1987 and 1994. To understand the role of these and other factors underlying the observed trends in income poverty it is necessary to look in detail at changes in the profile of households below the relative income thresholds, which is the subject of the next chapter.

Chapter 5

RISK AND INCIDENCE OF RELATIVE INCOME POVERTY

5.1 INTRODUCTION

In this chapter we analyse the risk and incidence of poverty using relative income poverty lines. The *risk* of poverty for any group is measured by the *proportion of that group* which actually falls below the relevant income standard. The *incidence* of poverty for the group is the *proportion of all those in poverty* who belong to that group. Groups which have a higher incidence of poverty than their share in the total population then face a higher than average risk of poverty; groups with a lower than average risk of poverty have a lower poverty incidence than their share of the total population. Using these measures we focus on the characteristics of low income households in 1994 in terms of their composition and labour force participation. We identify how the risks of relative income poverty have changed for different groups in the 1987 to 1994 period, and tease out how this helps to explain the overall trends in numbers below the income poverty lines described in the previous chapter. We also look at how these changes relate to earlier developments in the 1973 to 1987 period.

We begin (Section 5.2) by considering the relationship between poverty and some basic demographic characteristics (such as household composition, age and sex). Section 5.3 goes on to examine the trends in poverty risk and incidence classified by the labour force status of the household head. The main findings are drawn together in the concluding section 5.4. To simplify the presentation the results given in this chapter are based entirely on equivalence scale A, which is closest to the relativities implicit in the Irish social welfare system: the broad pattern of the results is not affected by the use of alternative scales B or C discussed in Chapter 4.

5.2 DEMOGRAPHIC CHARACTERISTICS: HOUSEHOLD TYPE, AGE AND SEX

To begin exploring the types of household falling below the relative income lines, Table 5.1 shows the demographic composition of households falling below the 50 per cent relative cut-off for the years 1973, 1980, 1987 and 1994 by broad category. Adult-only households formed about two-thirds of the poverty population in 1973; this had fallen sharply to under 40 per cent by 1987. The new data for 1994 show a reversal in this trend, with adult-only households accounting for 46 per cent of those below the 50 per cent income line in 1994. This is attributable entirely to an increase in the importance among the poor of households comprising a single adult, with the proportion of households below the 50 per cent line of this type doubling from 12 per cent to 26 per cent.

TABLE 5.1: COMPOSITION OF HOUSEHOLDS UNDER 50 PER CENT RELATIVE POVERTY LINE, 1973–94 (COMPOSITION OF *TOTAL* HOUSEHOLDS IN PARENTHESES)

	1973 HBS		1980 HBS		1987 ESRI		1994 LII	
Household type								
1 adult	32.2	(14.0)	29.5	(16.4)	12.1	(16.6)	25.4	(22.0)
2 adults	23.7	(19.9)	17.2	(20.2)	13.6	(18.5)	10.1	(20.2)
3 or more adults only	12.2	(19.6)	9.8	(14.5)	13.3	(20.3)	9.5	(18.1)
2 adults with children	13.8	(24.0)	22.3	(30.2)	38.3	(28.3)	21.3	(20.9)
Others with children	18.0	(22.5)	21.2	(18.6)	22.7	(16.4)	33.7	(19.0)
Total	100.0	(100)	100.0	(100)	100.0	(100)	100.0	(100)

Notes: Child = under 14 years of age; "others with children" includes single adults with children (most of whom are lone parents) and 3 or more adults with children. Equivalence scale 1/0.66/0.33.

The other striking change in the 1987 to 1994 period is the sharp fall in the share of two-adult households with children in the low income population. This is only partly because such households make up a smaller proportion of the population as a whole — they accounted for 28 per cent of the sample in 1987 but only 21 per cent by 1994. By contrast, other households with children increased in importance both in the sample as a whole but more particularly among those below the 50 per cent line. The poverty risks faced by these household types have therefore also changed. The way poverty risks have evolved is analysed using a more detailed household type categorisation in Table 5.2.

This table shows that the 1973 to 1987 period saw dramatic falls in the risks of poverty faced by single adult households and two-adult households. The new data for 1994, on the other hand, show a continued fall for two-adult households but a sharp increase in risk for one-adult ones. Turning to those with children, the risk for two-adult households with children was considerably higher in 1987 than it had been in 1973. The 1994 data show that the risk for two-adult households with one or two children peaked in 1987 and had fallen slightly by 1994. The risk for two-adult households with three children stayed roughly at the 1987 level by 1994 while for two adults plus four or more children there was some increase in risk. The risk for other households containing children has risen sharply, by 10 percentage points. The household types with the highest risks are now those comprising a single adult only, a couple with four or more children, and "other adults with children".

TABLE 5.2: TRENDS IN RISK OF POVERTY BY HOUSEHOLD TYPE AT 50 PER CENT RELATIVE POVERTY LINE, 1973–94

	1973 *HBS*	*1980* *HBS*	*1987* *ESRI*	*1994* *LII*
	% Below Line			
1 adult	42.2	30.2	11.9	21.4
2 adults	21.9	14.3	12.0	9.3
3 or more adults only	11.4	11.4	10.7	9.7
2 adults, 1 child	10.1	6.9	16.6	14.1
2 adults, 2 children	5.6	10.2	18.0	14.3
2 adults, 3 children	8.8	10.7	21.2	22.2
2 adults, 4+ children	16.3	23.2	35.6	38.2
Others with children	14.7	19.1	22.6	32.8
All households	18.3	16.8	17.5	18.5

Notes: Child = under 14 years of age; "others with children" includes single adults with children (most of whom are lone parents) and 3 or more adults with children. Equivalence scale 1/0.66/0.33.

The "other households with children" category comprises both single adults with children and three or more adults with children, but is in fact mostly made up of the latter. In 1994, about 85 per cent of the households in this category are three or more adults with children. It is important to recall however that the age cut-off for defining a child adopted here is 14, for comparability with the HBS, so many of these households are actually a couple with older children. Further investigation will be required as to why the risk for this group has increased so sharply since 1987.[1] As far as lone parents are concerned, this group was so small in 1973 and 1980 that risk figures from the HBS would not be reliable, but it is useful to look at them separately in the 1987 and 1994 surveys. The risk of falling below the 50 per cent income line for households comprising a single adult with children rose from about 30 per cent in 1987 to 57 per cent in 1994, and almost all these are lone parents (mostly mothers). Although still a relatively small group (less than 3 per cent of the sample), it does face a particularly high risk.

To see the impact of using a higher income line on poverty risks and composition, Table 5.3 compares the pattern seen with the 50 per cent line to that with the 60 per cent line in 1994. This shows that while poverty risks are, of course, higher with the 60 per cent line, the increase is greater for some household types than others. For single adult and two-adult households the risk more than doubles, with the risk for the former group now over 50 per cent. The increase for other household types is less, so households with one or two adults only account for 48 per cent of all those below the 60 per cent line, compared with 36 per cent of those below the 50 per cent line. Households of 2 adults with 4 or more children and "other households with children" continue to face relatively high risks with the 60 per cent line. (Among the latter, households of one adult with children again face a particularly high risk, with two-thirds falling below the 60 per cent line.)

---

[1] Of the households of this type falling below the 50 per cent line in 1994, about one-third are headed by someone in home duties and slightly fewer have an unemployed head.

TABLE 5.3: RISK AND COMPOSITION OF POVERTY BY HOUSEHOLD TYPE AT 50 AND 60 PER CENT RELATIVE POVERTY LINES, 1994

	Risk of Poverty		% of Poor	
	50% line	60% line	50% line	60% line
1 adult	21.4	51.7	25.4	32.9
2 adults	9.3	26.5	10.1	15.5
3 or more adults only	9.7	18.4	9.5	9.6
2 adults, 1 child	14.1	23.7	4.1	3.7
2 adults, 2 children	14.3	19.3	6.0	4.3
2 adults, 3 children	22.2	32.3	6.2	4.8
2 adults, 4+ children	38.2	48.0	5.0	3.3
Others with children	32.8	47.1	33.7	25.9
All households	18.5	34.6	100.0	100.0

A key factor in explaining the composition and risk changes between 1987 and 1994, in particular the sharp increase in risk for single-adult only households, is the changing relationship between the poverty lines and the rates paid under different social welfare programmes. A significant proportion of the single-adult households below the line in 1994 comprise an elderly person or a widow. This reflects the fact that the rate paid under non-contributory Old Age or Widow's Pension (including Living Alone Allowance) in 1994 was just below the 50 per cent line for a single person up until the mid-year rate increase, after which it was just above that level. In 1987, by contrast, the rate paid under these schemes was significantly higher than the 50 per cent line at that time. While mean equivalent income and thus the relative poverty lines rose by 51 per cent between 1987 and 1994, as we have seen, the rates paid under Old Age and Widow's Pensions (contributory or non-contributory) were increased by about 30 per cent over the period. This was a result of the strategy adopted of giving priority to increasing the lowest rates of social welfare, so that Unemployment Assistance and SWA rates rose by 60 per cent or more. Despite this, UA/SWA rates by 1994 were still just below the 50 per cent line, so although prioritising these rates will have made a major contribution towards the reduction in poverty gaps described in Chapter 4, it will not have had as much impact on the head-count with the 50 or 60 per cent lines.

Table 5.4 summarises the trends in poverty risk with the 50 per cent line as they affect adults (those aged 14 or over) and children. (Recall once again that children are defined as aged under 14, for comparability with the CSO's Household Budget Survey.) The 1973 to 1987 results showed increased risk for children at all three cut-offs. The new data for 1994 show the risk for children unchanged at the 40 per cent relative income cut-off but increasing at both the 50 per cent and 60 per cent lines. The risks for adults are much less volatile over the whole period, with the largest change being a rise in risk at the 60 per cent line of about 8 percentage points (as compared with a corresponding rise of 13 percentage points for children). Focusing on the 1987 to 1994 period, we see that the risk for adults, as for children, was unchanged at the 40 per cent line and increased at the 50 per cent and 60 per cent lines. In terms of the position of children versus adults, then, children remain at higher risk in 1994, but the gap between risks for children versus adults has narrowed somewhat since 1987, particularly with the 60 per cent line. The children in households below the relative income lines in 1994 are spread over households of differing size and composition, with 44 per cent in households comprising 3 or more adults with children, 15 per cent in households with only one adult, and 41 per cent in households of 2 adults with children. While the influences at work will require more study, the primary factor in bringing about the increase in risk for children over the period 1980–87 was the dramatic increase in unemployment, and the main reason why that risk remained so high in 1994 is that the unemployment rate, though falling, was still over 15 per cent.

TABLE 5.4: RISKS OF POVERTY FOR ADULTS AND CHILDREN, 1973–94

	1973 HBS	1980 HBS	1987 ESRI	1994 LII
Children	% Below Line[a]			
40% line	8.1	10.1	7.6	7.7
50% line	16.2	18.5	25.5	29.3
60% line	27.5	29.5	37.8	40.3
Adults				
40% line	7.4	7.7	6.5	6.5
50% line	15.1	15.2	16.1	17.9
60% line	24.4	25.4	26.5	31.9

[a] Equivalence scale 1/0.66/0.33.

A major contributor to the increase in risk for single adult households and for adults, already mentioned above, has been the change in the relative income position of the elderly. As noted in Callan, Nolan et al. (1989), increases in the real income of pensioners in the 1973 to 1987 period came from increased coverage under occupational pension schemes, and from greater coverage and higher rates under the social welfare pension schemes. During the 1987 to 1994 period, as we have seen, social welfare rates for pensioners were increased only slightly more than the rate of price inflation, and not in line with other incomes in the economy, with priority being given to raising the lowest rates of social welfare payments. Given this pattern, one might expect some deterioration in the relative income position of the elderly over the 1987 to 1994 period. Table 5.5 addresses this issue by focusing on the position of households headed by an elderly person. The dramatic fall in poverty risk for such households during the 1973 to 1987 period is clear. In the 1987 to 1994 period, the risk remained low at the 40 per cent and 50 per cent cut-offs, but rose very sharply at the 60 per cent cut off. The elderly living alone face a particularly high risk in 1994: two-thirds of the households below the 60 per cent line and headed by an elderly person are in fact single-person households.

TABLE 5.5: RISKS OF RELATIVE POVERTY FOR HOUSEHOLDS HEADED BY AN ELDERLY PERSON 1973–94

Relative Poverty Line[a]	*1973* *HBS*	*1980* *HBS*	*1987* *ESRI*	*1994* *LII*
	% Below Line			
40% line	12.9	7.1	3.6	3.2
50% line	30.9	24.4	7.2	9.8
60% line	44.0	46.6	20.9	41.5

[a] Equivalence scale 1/0.66/0.33.

Turning to risk by gender, Callan, Nolan et al. (1989) found that the relative income situation of female-headed households had improved during the 1973 to 1987 period, so that at the 40 per cent and 50 per cent relative income lines, female-headed households faced lower risks than households headed by a man or couple. At the 60 per cent line, the risk for female-headed households had declined relative to male- or couple-headed households, but remained slightly higher. During the 1987 to 1994 period, Table 5.6 shows that the relative position of female-headed households disimproved considerably with the 50 and 60 per cent lines. At both these lines the risk for female-headed households rose markedly, while that for male- or couple-headed households was little changed, so that by 1994 female-headed households are now at substantially higher risk than male- or couple-headed ones. At the 40 per cent line, on the other hand, the risk is still higher for a household headed by a man or couple. This is again linked to the increase in risk for the elderly with the 50 per cent and 60 per cent lines: almost half the female-headed households below the 60 per cent income line consist of an elderly woman living alone. The increase in numbers of lone parents and the risk of poverty facing them also contributed to this trend, but by 1994 only 15 per cent of the female-headed households below the 60 per cent line were lone parent households. The main factor behind the increase in risk for female-headed households is the fact that social welfare pensions rose less rapidly than the relative poverty lines: over 60 per cent of the female-headed households below the 60 per cent line in 1994 were in receipt of old age or widow's (contributory or non-contributory) pensions.

TABLE 5.6 RISKS OF RELATIVE POVERTY FOR HOUSEHOLDS HEADED BY MAN/COUPLE OR WOMAN, 1973–94

Relative Poverty Line[a]	Household Headed by:	1973 HBS	1980 HBS	1987 ESRI	1994 LII
40% line	Couple or Male	7.7	8.3	6.6	5.3
	Female	14.8	6.8	4.3	4.0
50% line	Couple or Male	15.7	15.6	18.0	16.8
	Female	29.3	22.4	8.9	24.0
60% line	Couple or Male	24.7	25.8	27.9	29.1
	Female	38.3	36.3	30.8	52.7

[a] Equivalence scale 1/0.66/0.33.

5.3 ECONOMIC CHARACTERISTICS: LABOUR FORCE STATUS

We now turn to the analysis of poverty risk and incidence on the basis of labour force status. In doing so, we follow conventional practice in categorising households by the labour force status of their head. (The household head is in most cases the same as the "household reference person" used in the 1994 survey as defined in Chapter 3.)[2] Over three-quarters of household heads in the 1994 survey are male, 23 per cent are female. Table 5.7 shows the composition of the households below the 50 per cent relative income line in 1994, and of the entire sample, together with the corresponding figures for 1987, 1980 and 1973. This shows that, as in 1987, households with an unemployed head make up the largest single group. However, households headed by a farmer make up a much smaller proportion of those below the 50 per cent line in 1994 than they did in 1987. The counterbalancing increase has been in the number of households below the line where the head is "in home duties", the term generally used in labour force analyses to describe working full-time in the home. From the composition of the sample as a whole we can see that this is not because the overall number of households of that type in the population has grown rapidly.

TABLE 5.7: COMPOSITION OF HOUSEHOLDS UNDER 50 PER CENT RELATIVE POVERTY LINE BY LABOUR FORCE STATUS OF HEAD OF HOUSEHOLD, 1973–94

Labour Force Status of Household Head	% of All Households Below Line[a]				% of All Households in Sample			
	1973 HBS	1980 HBS	1987 ESRI	1994 LII	1973 HBS	1980 HBS	1987 ESRI	1994 ESRI
Employee	9.0	10.3	8.2	6.2	42.4	47.1	38.6	37.5
Self-employed (excl. farmers)	3.6	3.5	4.8	6.7	6.5	6.8	7.5	8.5
Farmer	26.0	25.9	23.7	8.9	22.4	16.1	11.7	8.1
Unemployed	9.6	14.7	37.4	32.6	2.9	3.9	10.6	10.2
Ill/Disabled	10.2	9.3	11.1	9.5	4.5	3.3	6.0	4.0
Retired	17.0	18.9	8.1	10.5	10.6	13.7	14.5	18.3
Home Duties	24.6	17.4	6.7	25.5	10.7	9.1	11.1	13.5
Total	100.0	100.0	100.0	100.0	100.0	100.0	100.0	100.0

[a] Equivalence scale: 1/0.66/0.33.

---

[2] The household reference person was defined by Eurostat for the purpose of the ECHP as the owner or tenant of the accommodation, and where two or more people were equally responsible the oldest was taken. For comparability with results for previous years based on the household head (which did not employ this age criterion), where a female household reference person's husband was living in the household we took the husband as household head. The reference person was not the head in only 4.5 per cent of households.

Instead, as Table 5.8 shows, it comes about largely because the risk of falling below the 50 per cent line rose sharply between 1987 and 1994 for households headed by someone working in the home. We can also see that the risk facing households headed by an unemployed person was unchanged between 1987 and 1994 at this poverty line, while there was a pronounced fall for those headed by a farmer. Households with an unemployed head continue to face a much higher risk of falling below the 50 per cent line than others. The decreasing risk for households headed by a farmer is a reflection of the fact, already emphasised in Chapter 4, that the year to which the information on farm incomes in the 1987 ESRI survey applies was a particularly bad one. As far as the increase in risk for households headed by someone in home duties is concerned, this appears to relate to the factor identified earlier in discussing the increase in risk for single-adult households: the fact that the growth in social welfare old age and widow's pensions lagged behind that in mean incomes. More than half the households headed by someone in home duties and below the 60 per cent line have an elderly woman as head (most of these being an elderly woman living alone), and almost two-thirds are in receipt of social welfare old age or widow's pensions.

TABLE 5.8: RISKS OF RELATIVE POVERTY CLASSIFIED BY LABOUR FORCE STATUS OF HEAD OF HOUSEHOLD, 1973–94 (50 PER CENT RELATIVE POVERTY LINE)

Labour Force Status	1973 HBS	1980 HBS	1987 ESRI	1994 LII
	% Below Line[a]			
Employee	3.9	3.7	3.5	3.1
Self-employed	10.1	8.6	10.5	14.7
Farmer	21.2	27.0	32.8	20.4
Unemployed	61.9	63.1	57.2	59.4
Ill/Disabled	42.8	48.2	33.7	44.5
Retired	29.5	23.3	9.1	10.6
Home duties	42.2	32.2	9.8	34.9
Total	18.3	16.8	16.3	18.5

[a] Equivalence scale 1/0.66/0.33.

It is important to see whether this pattern of risk across labour force status types holds across other income poverty lines, so

Table 5.9 brings together the risk results for the 50 per cent line with those for the 40 per cent and 60 per cent lines. We see that at the 60 per cent line the gap between those headed by an unemployed person and those with a head who is ill/disabled or in home duties has narrowed. With the 40 per cent line there is much less variation in risk across labour force status types, the unemployed, self-employed and farmers all having a relatively high risk. The category "ill/disabled" includes both those not at work because of illness and those unable to work due to disability. While further work will be needed to assess the situation of those with disabilities, it is clear (even before their special needs are taken into account) that they face a very high risk of poverty, not much lower than households headed by an unemployed person; it is also worth noting that their risk has risen since 1987.

TABLE 5.9: RISKS OF POVERTY BY LABOUR FORCE STATUS OF HEAD OF HOUSEHOLD (40, 50 AND 60 PER CENT RELATIVE POVERTY LINE), 1994

Labour Force Status of HOH	Per cent of sample households	40% line[a] Risk (%)	50% line[a] Risk (%)	60% line[a] Risk (%)
Employee	37.5	0.7	3.1	7.5
Self-employed	8.5	9.3	14.7	19.0
Farmer	8.1	10.4	20.4	32.2
Unemployed	10.1	13.8	59.4	77.8
Ill/disabled	4.0	7.9	44.5	74.1
Retired	18.3	2.8	10.6	38.9
Home duties	13.5	6.3	34.9	71.3
All households	100.0	5.0	18.5	34.6

[a] Equivalence scale 1/0.66/0.33.

5.4 CONCLUSION

This chapter has analysed the pattern of risk and incidence of poverty in 1994 when households are categorised by some key characteristics: household composition type, and age, sex and labour force status of the household head. Comparison with 1987 shows a good deal of continuity, as would be expected, but also some important differences which will merit further investigation. The most striking changes were an increase in the risk of falling below half average income facing single-adult households, the elderly, female-headed households and households headed by someone in home duties — with a good deal of overlap between these groups — and a decline in the risk for farm households. The falling risk for farm households is directly attributable to the unusually bad year covered by the 1987 survey, but the evolution of social welfare rates for different categories of recipient *vis-à-vis* mean income for all households appears to have played a crucial role in the other elements of this pattern. Support rates for the elderly and widows were increased by a good deal less than mean incomes between 1987 and 1994, and as a result those relying entirely on means-tested old age or widow's pensions were on incomes at or about the 50 per cent benchmark by 1994, whereas in 1987 they had been above that level.

At the same time, as recommended by the Commission on Social Welfare, resources were concentrated on what had been the lowest social welfare rates in 1987 — UA and SWA — and these were increased substantially more rapidly than mean incomes. However, the scale of increase sufficed to bring them much closer to, but not quite up to, the 50 per cent relative income line. A major plank of social welfare strategy over the period thus will have had limited impact on reducing the numbers on UA or SWA falling below half average income, while the associated relative decline in the support provided to other groups will have increased the vulnerability of those groups. This helps to explain the overall pattern documented in Chapter 4, where the poverty measures taking the extent to which people fall below the 50 and 60 per cent income lines were stable or fell while the headcount of numbers below those lines rose. This brings out the importance of using those more complex summary measures as complements to simply "counting the poor". It is also important not to rely entirely on income in assessing the position of different households, and we turn in Chapter 6 to look at poverty risk and incidence when income is combined with information on deprivation indicators to identify those experiencing generalised deprivation due to lack of resources.

Chapter 6

LIFE-STYLE AND DEPRIVATION

6.1 INTRODUCTION

Poverty is now widely conceptualised in terms of exclusion from the life of a society because of a lack of resources, and being "excluded" in this context is generally taken to mean experiencing various forms of what that society regards as serious deprivation, both material and social. In relying on income to make statements about poverty defined in this way, it is necessary to assume that those falling below the specified income poverty line are not able to participate fully in the life of the community. This cannot be simply taken for granted, however, it requires validation. Assessing the validity of income as a "marker" for exclusion involves a comparison with direct measures of deprivation. This in turn requires that we arrive at indicators of deprivation suitable for this purpose. Considerable progress in that direction has been made in our earlier work using the 1987 survey (Callan, Nolan et al., 1989, Callan, Nolan and Whelan, 1993; Nolan and Whelan, 1996). In this chapter we apply the methods of employing non-monetary indicators developed in that work to the new data for 1994, and compare the results with 1987.

In Chapter 2, we identified the key issues to be addressed in using indicators of deprivation in measuring poverty as follows:

1. How to select items that are suitable to serve as deprivation indicators.

2. How to take into account the role of tastes versus resource constraints as determinants of living patterns.

3. How to aggregate deprivation items into a summary index or set of dimensions or otherwise to make use of the information they contain.

4. How to select a particular cut-off to distinguish the poor from the non-poor, either on the basis of deprivation scores or using

both deprivation and income criteria; and fundamentally, how to elucidate the ways in which the observed deprivation/income pattern comes about.

We now proceed to describe the non-monetary indicators available to us in the 1987 and 1994 surveys, and the way our approach tackles these issues in using this information to measure exclusion due to lack of resources.

6.2 LIFE-STYLE AND DEPRIVATION INDICATORS IN 1987 AND 1994

Individual Indicators

In the 1987 ESRI survey respondents were given a list of 20 items or activities, most of which had been selected for inclusion in the survey on the basis that they had proved useful in previous studies such as Townsend (1979) and Mack and Lansley (1985) using UK data. These indicators apply across all household types.[1] Following Mack and Lansley (1985), respondents were asked which items they believed were "necessities — that is things which every household (or person) should be able to have and that nobody should have to do without", which items they did not themselves have/avail of, and which of these they would like to have but had to do without because of lack of money.

In 1994, 19 of these items were included in the survey. The twentieth, an item relating to heating, was asked in this format in both surveys but the wording was sufficiently different to make direct comparisons misleading.[2] In 1994 the information collected on the range of items was restricted to possession and affordability, no information being collected in relation to perceived necessity. In addition, in 1987 most adult household members were asked separately about the list of items, but in 1994 this question was on the household rather than individual questionnaire and

---

[1] Some items applying only to particular types of households — for example, those with children — have been employed in other studies, but the complications involved in using them in our view outweigh the possible benefits.

[2] In 1987 the question was whether the respondent had "heating for the living room when it is cold", while in 1994 it was a much broader one on availability of "adequate heating for your home", to which a much higher proportion responded in the negative.

thus we have responses only from the household reference person. In comparing 1987 and 1994 we therefore use the responses of the household head in 1987 and those of the household reference person in 1994 — knowing that in most cases the reference person is also what would conventionally be termed the household head, as discussed in Chapter 5. Analysis of the responses of spouses in the 1987 survey across the various items suggested that there was not much systematic difference between husbands' and their wives' responses (Cantillon and Nolan, 1996), so in assessing the situation of the household the choice between them should in any case make little difference.

In Table 6.1 we compare the sample responses on possession/ lack of the nineteen items and subjective assessments of affordability for Ireland in 1987 and 1994. This shows a substantial improvement in living standards between the two years. Looking first at basic items of food and clothing, a significant improvement is seen for all these except new not second-hand clothes. By 1994, the percentage lacking items such as two pairs of strong shoes, a meal without meat, fish or chicken every second day, a warm waterproof overcoat or two pairs of strong shoes is down to about half the 1987 figure. Focusing on enforced lack, a similar reduction in levels of deprivation can be observed. In 1987 the numbers experiencing what respondents considered to be enforced deprivation of these items ranged from 8 per cent to 13 per cent of the sample, while by 1994 the corresponding range was 5 to 8 per cent. (This still constitutes a significant number reporting enforced lack of very basic items which many people take for granted, of course, but the decline over the period is marked.)

Significant improvement in living standards was also observed in relation to a range of items falling into non-essential category. The most dramatic change relates to telephone ownership where the number lacking a telephone declines from about one in two to one in four. The corresponding figure for central heating falls from 45 per cent to 28 per cent. (These trends are consistent with the information available from external sources on ownership of these items in the population).[3] The number not buying presents for friends and family once a year and not having a holiday are also

---

[3] Telecom estimate that telephone penetration went from 54 per cent of households in 1987 to 75 per cent in 1994. Similarly, Forfas report the estimated level of households with central heating in 1993 at 70 per cent which compares with our figure for 1994 of 72 per cent.

down substantially. Other items such as ability to save, car ownership, a daily newspaper and a hobby or leisure activity show
much smaller falls. When we focus on enforced absence we find
that the level of deprivation, defined as non-possession of items
because of (self-assessed) inability to afford them, again falls for
most of these items. For example, the percentage not having a
telephone and stating that this is because they could not afford it
falls from 31 per cent in 1987 to 14 per cent in 1994.

TABLE 6.1: INDICATORS OF STYLE OF LIVING AND DEPRIVATION IN
1987 AND 1994 SAMPLES

	% Lacking		% Enforced Lack	
	1987	*1994*	*1987*	*1994*
New Not Second-hand Clothes*	10	10	8	8
A Meal with Meat, Fish or Chicken Every Second Day*	13	6	9	5
A Warm Waterproof Overcoat*	13	8	8	6
Two Pairs of Strong Shoes*	16	8	11	7
A Roast or its Equivalent Once a Week*	24	15	13	8
A Week's Annual Holiday Away From Home	68	55	49	40
To be able to Save Some of One's Income Regularly	57	53	55	48
A Daily Newspaper	45	43	16	14
Telephone	48	23	31	14
A Hobby or Leisure Activity*	33	32	12	12
Central Heating	45	28	30	18
Presents For Family and Friends Once a Year*	24	14	13	9
Car*	38	35	22	18
Bath or Shower*	9	5	7	4
Indoor Toilet*	7	4	6	3
Washing Machine*	20	14	10	5
Refrigerator*	5	2	3	1
Colour Television	20	5	11	2
A Dry — Damp Free Dwelling*	10	9	9	8

* Regarded as a necessity, and possessed, by a majority of the sample in
1987.

The remaining items relate to housing conditions and household
durables and the pattern of improvement in living standards is

sustained. Most strikingly the number of households lacking a colour TV falls sharply from 20 per cent to 5 per cent. The numbers lacking a bath or shower falls from 9 per cent to 5 per cent, a dry damp-free dwelling from 10 to 9 per cent, an indoor toilet from 7 to 4 per cent and a refrigerator from 5 to 2 per cent. Focusing on enforced lack, we find that while in 1987 the percentage doing without these items because they could not afford them ranged from 3 to 11 per cent, by 1994 the corresponding range ran from 1 to 5 per cent.

Four additional items were included in both surveys, but not in the format of has/lacks, can/cannot afford which was employed for the nineteen items just examined. Two of these were asked in 1987 only of the household manager, defined as the person who buys most of the groceries for the household. For 1994 we therefore use the responses of the person most likely to be in that position.[4] The four items were as follows:

1. Whether there was a day during the previous two weeks when the household manager did not have a substantial meal at all, from getting up to going to bed.

2. Whether the household manager had to go without heating during the last year through lack of money i.e., having to go without a fire on a cold day or to go to bed early to keep warm or light the fire late because of lack of coal/fuel.

3. Whether the household head has not had an afternoon or evening out in the last fortnight "something that costs money", and this was stated to be because they did not have enough money.

4. Whether the household head or spouse report experiencing debt problems arising from ordinary living expenses or having to avail of charity.

It is the presence of these items that would potentially indicate deprivation whereas for the 19 items in Table 6.1 it was, of course, *absence* that would do so. These additional items, although not available in the preferred "has/lacks, can/cannot afford" format,

---

[4] A direct question identifying the household manager was not included in 1994, and so we use the responses of the household reference person unless that is a man with a spouse living in the household, in which case his wife's responses are taken.

nevertheless proved particularly valuable in the 1987 survey and are incorporated in the analysis here for that reason. For items 2 and 3 the question explicitly states that experiencing the problem is to be attributed to lack of money and for the other two the nature of the item makes it overwhelmingly likely that this is the case. We will, therefore, take it that these represent what respondents would themselves consider to be enforced deprivation in all cases.

TABLE 6.2: ADDITIONAL INDICATORS OF LIFE-STYLE AND DEPRIVATION IN 1987 AND 1994 SAMPLES

	1987	*1994*
	% of Households	
Had a day in the last two weeks without a substantial meal	4.5	3.8
Had to go without heating during the last year through lack of money	6.6	8.3
Unable to afford afternoon or evening out in previous 2 weeks	15.7	12.3
Debt problems arising from ordinary living expenses	14.5	12.3

From Table 6.2 we can see that for three of the four items there was a small decline in the percentage in the sample experiencing that particular form of deprivation — similar to the general pattern for the 19 items seen in Table 6.1. The exception is "having to go without heat", where a small increase in the percentage affected was reported .

Overall, then, for the sample as a whole there has been a clear trend towards reduced levels of deprivation with the range of non-monetary indicators available to us for 1987 and 1994. We now go on to employ these indicators in constructing summary indices of deprivation and then in examining the different dimensions of deprivation, along the lines implemented in our previous research based on the 1987 survey.

Summary Deprivation Indices

From the set of items available in the surveys, how should one select and aggregate items to measure deprivation? In their work with UK data, Townsend and Mack and Lansley both constructed summary deprivation indices with a sub-set of the life-style items on which they had information. Mack and Lansley selected items as indicators of deprivation on the basis that they were widely viewed as necessities, whereas Townsend focused on items or activities actually possessed/pursued by a majority. Our own results for Ireland with the 1987 survey (e.g., in Callan, Nolan et al., 1989, Chapter 8) showed that two groups of items were possessed by the vast majority of households and were also considered to be necessities by a substantial majority. One of these groups related to basic items of food and clothing, the other to housing and household durables. There were, however, several items which were viewed as necessities by a majority of the sample but possessed by only a minority, and vice versa. Only 43 per cent of respondents were able to save but 88 per cent thought being able to do so was a necessity, while 80 per cent of households had a colour TV but only 37 per cent thought it was a necessity. As a consequence, the basis on which indicators of deprivation are chosen — whether on the basis of *views* or on the actual possession — can make a difference. The items involved may in any case relate to rather different aspects or dimensions of deprivation, and simply adding them in a single index without taking that into account may not be the most appropriate procedure. We therefore look first at how similar summary indices could be constructed from the items in our sample, but proceed to an examination of the relationships between the items and the implications for the construction of deprivation indices.

In our initial analysis of the indicators in the 1987 survey, we constructed summary indices using the 14 items, from the set of 20 on which we had full information, which were both regarded as a necessity by a majority of the sample and possessed by a majority. A "lack" index was constructed by attributing a score of 1 for each item which the respondent states they do not have, and an "enforced lack" index scored 1 for each item lacked because of what the respondent said was inability to afford it. Each index had a minimum score of 0 and a maximum score of 14. For 1994 we have to exclude the heating item because of non-comparability, as already mentioned, but can construct the equivalent 13-item index. (The items included are marked with an asterisk in Table 6.1.) Table 6.3 shows the distribution of scores on the 13-item lack and enforced lack indices in both 1994 and 1987.[5] We see that for

---

[5] Excluding the heating item in fact makes virtually no difference to the results for 1987, but we use here results for the 13-item index rather than

both the lack and the enforced lack index there has been a substantial increase between 1987 and 1994 in the percentage of
households with scores of zero, and a corresponding fall in the
percentage with scores between 3-9.

TABLE 6.3: DISTRIBUTION OF SCORES ON 13-ITEM LACK AND
ENFORCED LACK SUMMARY INDEX

Score	% of Households			
	Lack		Enforced Lack	
	1987	1994	1987	1994
0	30.7	40.5	51.3	61.6
1-2	35.3	35.7	29.5	25.4
3-5	23.7	17.1	14.4	9.0
6-9	8.7	5.1	4.6	3.9
10-13	1.6	1.6	0.3	0.1
All	100	100	100	100

Alternatively, one can simply construct an aggregate index with
all 23 items on which we have information for both years. Concentrating on enforced lack, in such a summary deprivation index a
household scores 1 for each of the 19 items in Table 6.1 which
they do not have because they cannot afford it, and one for each of
the four additional aspects of deprivation in Table 6.2 which they
do experience. The pattern of scores on the index for both 1987
and 1994 on this 23-item enforced lack index is shown in Table
6.4. The percentage scoring zero again increased considerably,
from 21 per cent in 1987 to 32 per cent in 1994. On the other
hand, the percentage of households experiencing an enforced lack
of more than four of items declined from 41 to 27 per cent. The
average number of items in relation to which households experienced enforced deprivation fell from 3.64 in 1987 to 2.54 in 1994,
a reduction of just over one quarter.

those for the 14-item one given in Callan, Nolan et al., (1989) Table 8.2 p.
115.

TABLE 6.4: DISTRIBUTION OF SCORES ON 23-ITEM ENFORCED LACK SUMMARY INDEX

Score	% of Households	
	1987	1994
0	21.5	32.0
1-3	37.0	41.2
4-6	22.1	16.1
7-9	11.7	5.4
10-12	4.6	3.0
13-15	2.1	1.9
16 or More	0.9	0.4
All	100.0	100.00
Mean Level of Deprivation	3.64	2.54

Dimensions of Deprivation

While analysis of the 13- and 23-item indices provides useful information, focusing on such a summary index might not be satisfactory. As we have emphasised in earlier work, simply aggregating items in a single index ignores the fact that different items may reflect different dimensions of deprivation, so adding them together may lose valuable information. In analysing the data from the 1987 survey we sought to systematically examine the manner in which items cluster into distinct groups in order to identify dimensions of deprivation. In order to do so we applied factor analysis to the 24 items available in 1987, focusing on enforced absence in the case of the 20 items on which we had subjective assessments of affordability. In attempting to develop a measure of deprivation appropriate to our conception of poverty (as involving a failure, due to lack of resources, to meet what are seen to be minimum standards in the society) we seek to establish the extent to which the enforced absence of a particular item reflects what Ringen (1987) refers to as a state of generalised deprivation and what Coates and Silburn (1970) termed an inter-related network of deprivation.

The first stage in the analysis, before attempting to select items that would be appropriate as indicators of such generalised deprivation, is to examine systematically the range of deprivation items to see whether the items cluster into distinct groups. Factor analysis enable us to identify such clusters of interrelated variables. Each factor or dimension is defined by those items that are more highly correlated with each other than with the other items. Our analysis of the 1987 data identified three dimensions of deprivation:

1. Basic life-style deprivation — consisting of basic items such as food and clothes.

2. Secondary life-style deprivation — consisting of items such as a car, telephone and leisure activities.

3. Housing deprivation — consisting of items related to housing quality and facilities

In order to make comparisons between the 1987 and 1994 surveys, we first wish to establish whether the structure of deprivation has remained unchanged. In Table 6.5 we compare the results of factor analysis at both points in time for the 23 items common to the two surveys.[6]

We can see that there is a striking similarity between the clustering of the deprivation indicators in the two surveys. The basic deprivation dimension is clearly identified in both cases: a range of items relating to debt, food and clothing contribute in almost equal measure to this dimension. The housing dimension which emerges at both times is dominated by the bath/shower and indoor toilet items but also includes a range of household durables. The secondary dimension is dominated by items such as holidays, a car, a telephone, central heating and being able to save. In the analysis of the 1987 data our concern to ensure that our measure of basic deprivation reflected generalised deprivation of the kind appropriate to a measure of poverty led us to avoid including items in this index which, while having their highest loading on this factor, had loadings on other factors which were not a great deal lower. It is of course possible that the composition of the basic deprivation index might change over time, so that one would need to delete, or more plausibly, to add items. An inspection of the results in Table 6.5 suggest that none of the items employed in

---

[6] The factor analysis results reported here for 1987 are slightly different from those previously reported because they are based on a general factor analytic procedure rather than that specifically for dichotomous items. This has little effect on the pattern of results but produces rather lower coefficients across all dimensions.

TABLE 6.5: CONVENTIONAL ROTATED FACTOR ANALYSIS SOLUTION
FOR LIFE-STYLE DEPRIVATION ITEMS

	Basic Life-Style Dimension		Secondary Dimension		Housing and Household Durables	
	1987	1994	1987	1994	1987	1994
Basic Dimension						
Go Without Heat	0.63	0.66	0.12	0.22	-0.10	0.08
Go Without Substantial Meal	0.61	0.68	-0.05	0.01	0.04	0.03
Debt/Charity	0.58	0.47	0.15	0.28	-0.10	-0.13
New not Second-Hand Clothes	0.58	0.66	0.22	0.26	0.13	0.05
Meal with Meat, Chicken or Fish	0.59	0.53	0.24	0.05	0.22	0.35
A Warm Waterproof Overcoat	0.55	0.52	0.13	0.29	0.23	0.12
Two Pairs of Strong Shoes	0.58	0.62	0.17	0.28	0.20	0.10
A Roast or its Equivalent Once a Week	0.46	0.60	0.38	0.14	0.16	0.17
Housing/Durables Dimension						
Bath or Shower	0.11	0.08	-0.09	-0.05	0.84	0.86
Indoor Toilet	0.11	0.04	-0.13	-0.07	0.84	0.83
Washing Machine	-0.02	0.04	0.30	0.20	0.45	0.42
Refrigerator	0.07	0.26	0.07	-0.13	0.44	0.38
Colour Television	0.02	-0.05	0.24	0.19	0.43	0.32
A Dry Damp Free Dwelling	0.15	0.12	0.21	0.37	0.31	0.38
Secondary Dimension						
Annual Holiday Away from Home	0.08	0.20	0.68	0.63	0.04	-0.03
To be Able to Save Some of One's Income Regularly	0.17	0.23	0.58	0.55	0.10	0.04
Daily Newspaper	0.18	0.35	0.52	0.33	0.09	0.02
Telephone	0.04	0.16	0.59	0.49	0.19	0.22
A Hobby or Leisure Activity	0.25	0.35	0.46	0.45	-0.08	-0.09
Central Heating	0.07	0.06	0.52	0.61	0.23	0.38
Present for Friends and Family Once a Year	0.32	0.55	0.48	0.28	0.08	0.03
Car	0.14	0.16	0.53	0.54	0.05	0.03
Able to Afford an Afternoon or Evening Out in Previous Two Weeks	0.20	0.31	0.43	0.42	-0.03	-0.09

relation to the 1987 data need to be deleted while the only serious candidate for inclusion is being able to afford presents for friends and family once a year.

Our analysis for 1994 thus confirms that it is sensible to continue to distinguish three dimensions instead of simply aggregating items across the three factors into a summary index. On the basis of the information available from the factor analysis together with the information on social perceived necessities and the additional criteria we have imposed, we can construct separate indices for enforced lack of basic, housing and secondary deprivation. The distribution of scores on the three indices is shown in Table 6.6. Focusing first on basic deprivation we find that the number experiencing an enforced lack of at least 1 item has fallen from 33 per cent in 1987 to 25 per cent in 1994, and the number lacking 1-4 items has fallen from 29 per cent to 22 per cent. Declining levels of deprivation are also seen for the housing dimension: in 1987, 26 per cent of households suffered an enforced lack of at least one of these items while the corresponding figure for 1994 was 15 per cent. Improved living standards are observed not only in the case of the kinds of social perceived necessities incorporated in the basic and housing deprivation indices but also in the case of the non-essential items which make up the secondary index. For this index the proportion of households experiencing no enforced deprivation rises from one-quarter to one-third, and the percentage of households deprived of 4 or more items drops from 30 per cent to 19 per cent. The average decline in scores is in fact very similar across the three indices: the mean score on each index in 1994 is about three-quarters the corresponding 1987 figure.

Our confidence in these measures will be affected by our assessment of their reliability. Fundamentally, reliability concerns the extent to which a procedure yields the same results on repeated trials. By far the most popular measure of reliability is Cronbach's coefficient alpha, and in Appendix 3 this measure is described and results compared for 1987 and 1994 for the overall 23 item summary index and the basic, housing and secondary dimensions. The values found in each year are once again strikingly similar. These results suggest that, particularly in relation to the overall and basic dimensions, our estimate of deprivation at both points in time would be very similar if any alternative set of indicators from the potentially infinite set of indicators tapping basic deprivation had been chosen. Evidence is also presented to show that neither the addition of comparable indicators, nor the deletion of any one of our current indicators, would substantially alter the conclusions we are likely to reach regarding the determinants and consequences of the dimensions of deprivation reflected in our indices.

TABLE 6.6: DISTRIBUTION OF SCORES ON BASIC, HOUSING AND SECONDARY LIFE-STYLE DIMENSIONS IN 1987 AND 1994 SAMPLES

Score*	Basic Deprivation (% of Households)		Housing Deprivation (% of Households)		Secondary Deprivation (% of Households)	
	1987	1994	1987	1994	1987	1994
0	67.2	74.9	74.0	84.7	24.2	33.5
1	15.1	12.6	15.0	10.1	17.1	20.2
2	7.0	4.6	6.0	3.1	16.0	15.3
3	4.1	2.6	3.0	1.4	13.4	11.8
4	3.1	1.7	1.2	0.6	10.7	7.5
5	1.9	1.7	0.7	0.2	8.4	4.9
6	0.6	1.0	0.1	—	5.1	4.2
7 or more	1.1	1.0	—	—	5.2	2.6
Total	100.0	100.0	100.0	100.0	100.0	100.0
Mean Score	0.75	0.58	0.45	0.34	2.44	1.86

* There are 8 items in the basic index, 6 in the housing index and 9 in the secondary index

6.3 INCOME, DEPRIVATION AND POVERTY

Combining Income and Deprivation Criteria

In this section we combine information on income and non-monetary indicators of deprivation in a manner which is consistent with our definition of poverty as *exclusion* arising from lack of resources. We thus follow through on the conclusion that if poverty is defined in this manner the poor must be identified using both deprivation *and* an income criterion. In doing so we are following Mack and Lansley in not taking respondents' own assessments in relation to enforced absence entirely at face value.

In seeking to identify those excluded due to a lack of resources we have to decide how best to use the indicators of deprivation and the income data available to us. As far as deprivation is concerned, one option would be to use the full set of 23 indicators on which we have information. This could involve simply using the summary index constructed from all the items, where absence of any item adds 1 to the household's score. Alternatively, we could follow Hallerod's Swedish study (1995) and construct a weighted index, where each item is weighted by the proportion in the sample regarding it as a necessity. In that way, all the items contribute to the deprivation measure but those whose absence is likely to be most severely felt add more to the index. However, some of the items included by Hallerod were neither possessed nor regarded as necessities by a majority of the sample. While we can see some logic in including such items in a measure of living standards, they do not appear to us to have a role to play — even with a low weighting — as indicators of generalised deprivation. Our aim, as spelt out earlier, is to measure inability to afford socially defined necessities: knowing that a household cannot afford an item regarded as a necessity by only 10 per cent of the population (such as access to a summer cottage, in Hallerod's Swedish sample) tells us something about that household's living standards but nothing at all about its ability to obtain such necessities.

The second option, followed by Townsend and by Mack and Lansley, is to select the sub-set of items possessed by a majority (Townsend) or regarded as a necessity by a majority (Mack and Lansley) as suitable to represent deprivation, and aggregate those in an index. Indeed, as we have demonstrated earlier, both these criteria can be applied together to produce a 13-item summary deprivation index for our sample. However, the fundamental objection to such a procedure is that the results of our factor analysis clearly show that these items cluster into different dimensions, so simply selecting items regarded as necessities/possessed by a majority and adding them across these dimensions fails to take this into account.

Each dimension contains important information about lifestyles and living standards, but here, given our objective, we concentrate on what we have termed the basic dimension. The items in the basic deprivation index clearly represented socially perceived necessities when views were sought in the 1987 survey as to which were "things that every household should be able to have and that nobody should have to do without": there is every reason to believe this was still the case in 1994. In both 1987 and 1994 these items are possessed by most people, they reflect rather basic aspects of current material deprivation, and they cluster together, which lends support to the notion that they are useful as indicators of the underlying generalised deprivation we are trying to measure. Most of the items in the secondary dimension, on the other hand, are not overwhelmingly regarded as necessities. (Less than 60 per cent on average saw them as necessities in 1987, as against an average of over 80 per cent for the items in the "basic" set.) The housing and durables items are possessed by most people and regarded as necessities by almost everyone (except for the TV). However, we have seen that in 1987 they did not relate to the current resources and extent of exclusion of the household in the same way as the basic items. The fact that they do not cluster with the basic items itself means that rather different households and causal processes are involved. Deprivation in terms of housing and related durables appears to be a product of very specific factors, and so the housing items, though providing valuable information about one important aspect of living standards, are not satisfactory as indicators of current generalised exclusion (Nolan and Whelan, 1996).

We therefore proceed by concentrating on the basic index. This is not because we wish to prescribe in a normative fashion a hierarchy in which people *should* satisfy their needs, or to focus exclusively on a particular set of items. Rather, the respondents' evaluations, the results of the factor analysis, and the analysis of the relationship between the different items and household resources leads us to believe that these are the best indicators available to us of the generalised underlying deprivation we are trying to measure. The first stage in identifying households that are excluded because of a lack of resources is therefore to look at scores on the 8-item index of enforced basic deprivation. Using an unchanged set of items in making comparisons between 1987 to 1994 could itself be criticised, in that the notion that expectations and perceptions of needs will change over time as general living standards rise is central to a relative conception of poverty. Two points are relevant here. First, some of the basic items we employ are broad rather than specific, and respondents' interpretations of what is entailed will probably change over time — for example, what is taken to constitute going without heating or a "substantial meal" or going into debt to meet "everyday expenses". Secondly, over a longer period one would certainly want to leave open the possibility of incorporating further items which through changing attitudes and expectations "become necessities", and this could be done by repeated monitoring of views in the population as to which items from a broad range constitute necessities. We do not have such information in our 1994 survey, though it is hoped to include it in a future wave of the European Community Household Panel in Ireland. For the present, we therefore rely on the same set of basic items as in 1987, but combine this with income lines which reflect changes in average income over time. Even over the relatively short seven-year span covered here this does probably represent if anything a conservative measure.

In assessing whether lack of a basic item is attributable to what would generally be considered insufficient resources, respondents' own assessments as to whether they were doing without the item because they could not afford it (information available for the five of the eight items in the basic index) is helpful but not sufficient. These responses apply individual rather than societal standards to what constitutes "enforced", and this gives rise to two concerns in this context. The first is that some of the households that lack basic items but say this is by choice may have grown accustomed to doing without, or may be reluctant to admit they cannot afford something most people have, whereas by societal standards they are doing without because of lack of resources. The second is that, conversely, some of those reporting enforced basic deprivation are on relatively high incomes, and by societal standards would be regarded as able to afford the item.

Enforcement owning to lack of resources needs to relate to societal rather than simply individual standards and expectations and needs to be taken into account directly if the poverty measure is to be fully consistent with the definition. This provides the rationale for focusing on both deprivation and relatively low incomes. Such a focus was justified by Ringen in the following terms:

> A state of general deprivation cannot be measured with either resource indicators or way of life indicators alone. . . . Resource indicators alone can only say something about the probability of deprivation in way of life. Low income, for example, may represent only a temporary and atypical situation which does not force the person in question to change his life style — he may for a while live off savings — and there may be ways of avoiding a life in deprivation in spite of low income, such as to live on someone else's income. To ascertain poverty we need to identify directly the consequences we normally expect to follow from low income. On the other hand, to rely on way of life indicators alone, that

is, to go all out for direct measurement, is also insufficient since people may live as if they were poor without being poor . . . We need to establish not only that people live as if they were poor but that they do so because they do not have the means to avoid it. (Ringen, 1987, pp. 161-162).

We will therefore identify households as excluded because of lack of resources only when they are reporting enforced lack of basic items *and* are on low income. But what constitutes low income? Rather than seek to derive an income threshold, the use of a range of income lines at this stage allows us to see the consequences of varying the income criterion for the numbers and types of household identified as poor. For this purpose we employ relative income lines derived from average disposable equivalent income, as in Chapters 4 and 5, namely 40, 50 and 60 per cent of the mean.

Combining Income and Deprivation Criteria: The Results

Table 6.7 shows the percentage of households in the sample falling below each of the relative income thresholds (using equivalence scale A as described in Chapter 4) *and* experiencing enforced deprivation of at least one basic item, for 1987 and 1994. In 1987 this ranged from 3 per cent using the 40 per cent income line to 16 per cent using the 60 per cent line. In 1994 the corresponding range was 2 per cent to 15 per cent. The table also shows the percentage below each income line and reporting enforced lack of 2 or more basic items. We see that in 1987 the range meeting these income and deprivation criteria is now from 2 per cent to 11 per cent, while for 1994 the corresponding range is from 1.7 per cent to 9 per cent. In each case there has been a marginal fall in the percentage below the relative income lines and experiencing basic deprivation. It will be recalled from Chapter 4 that the percentage of households falling below the 40 per cent income line fell, but (with equivalence scale A) the percentage below the 50 and particularly the 60 per cent lines rose between 1987 and 1994. Thus, combining these relative lines with a deprivation criterion held fixed from 1987 to 1994 gives quite a different picture to the income lines alone.

TABLE 6.7: PERCENTAGE OF HOUSEHOLDS BELOW RELATIVE
INCOME THRESHOLDS AND EXPERIENCING BASIC DEPRIVATION IN
1987 AND 1994 SAMPLES

	% Below Income Line and:			
	Experiencing Enforced Basic Deprivation		*Experiencing Enforced Lack of Two or More Items*	
Relative Income Line	*1987*	*1994*	*1987*	*1994*
40% line	3.3	2.4	2.0	1.7
50% line	9.8	8.9	6.6	6.0
60% line	16.0	14.9	10.7	9.0

We saw earlier in the chapter that, for the sample as a whole, scores
on the basic deprivation index — like those for the housing and
secondary indices — fell quite sharply between 1987 and 1994. The
numbers below the relative income lines and experiencing basic
deprivation have fallen by rather less. Clearly the rise in the percentage simply below the 50 and 60 per cent lines, before taking
deprivation scores into account, is an important part of the explanation. The percentage of households falling below the 60 per cent
income line (with equivalence scale A) rose sharply, from 28.5 per
cent in 1987 to 34.7 per cent in 1994, so the fact that the percentage
below that line and experiencing basic deprivation fell over the
same period is itself a reflection of a substantial decline in basic
deprivation. In fact, about 60 per cent of the households below that
income line in 1987 were experiencing basic deprivation, whereas
in 1994 this was true of only 45 per cent of the households below
the same relative line. Another element, however, is that the decline
in deprivation scores was more pronounced among those *not* below
the relative income lines. The mean score on the basic deprivation
index for those below the 60 per cent income line fell from 1.67 in
1987 to 1.18 in 1994, a decline of 30 per cent. The mean score for
those above that income line was 0.56 in 1987, and by 1994 had
fallen by over 50 per cent, to 0.26.

It is essential to emphasise once again at this point that the
presence or absence of a *particular* item in itself is not crucial.
The set of items measured is intended to serve as an indicator of
pervasive exclusion from ordinary living patterns — what Ringen
describes as a state of general deprivation — which is the latent
or underlying variable one is trying to measure. On conceptual
grounds, we would argue that genuinely enforced deprivation of

even one socially defined necessity should be sufficient to indicate such pervasive exclusion. Given the way in which the basic index has been constructed — the nature of the items themselves, the fact that the factor analysis showed that they cluster together, and that only subjectively assessed enforced lack is counted — and that an income criterion is also to be applied, we would argue that even a score of 1 on that index should be employed to indicate generalised deprivation.

Table 6.8 shows which items are in fact lacked by those experiencing basic deprivation and having an income below the 50 per cent line, and those between the 50 and 60 per cent lines, for both 1987 and 1994. The percentage lacking specific items is in some cases higher in 1994 than in 1987 and in some cases lower, but the results provide a graphic perspective on the living standards of the households concerned. For example, in 1994 over half of households below the 50 per cent line and experiencing basic deprivation were found to have severe debt problems. The household manager reported food problems in almost one-quarter, and heat difficulties in almost half these cases. About 40 per cent could not afford new clothes, 34 per cent could not afford two pairs of strong shoes and one-quarter a warm waterproof coat, one in three were deprived of a roast or equivalent and one in four a meal with chicken, meat or fish every second day.

TABLE 6.8: NATURE OF BASIC DEPRIVATION FOR HOUSEHOLDS AT DIFFERENT INCOME LEVELS AND LACKING AT LEAST ONE BASIC ITEM, 1987 AND 1994 SAMPLES

	Households Experiencing Basic Deprivation and			
	Below the 50% Line		*Between the 50% and 60% Lines*	
	% Lacking Item			
	1987	*1994*	*1987*	*1994*
Debt	54.5	56.9	44.0	33.2
Went without main meal	17.0	23.4	13.8	17.3
Went without heat	27.4	46.6	23.7	38.1
Enforced lack of:				
New clothes	33.6	38.3	22.3	41.4
Two pairs of shoes	43.7	33.9	36.2	37.2
Warm overcoat	24.4	28.5	31.7	25.7
Roast or equivalent once a week	44.7	38.4	37.2	33.3
Meal with meat, fish or equivalent	39.3	24.1	29.7	21.4

The Impact on Composition of Income and Deprivation

We have argued that the application of criteria in terms of both basic deprivation and current income serves to identify a set of households that merit the description "poor" in accordance with the Townsend definition, i.e., are excluded because of a lack of resources. Does applying these income-plus-deprivation criteria rather than purely income cut-offs make much difference to the composition of the group involved? In other words, are different types of household identified as poor? This is crucial, since it will indicate the extent to which income lines alone could potentially mislead policy-makers as to the main types of household towards which their efforts should be directed, and will also affect how we understand poverty and the processes generating it. In 1987, the number below the 50 per cent income line was almost exactly the same as the number below the 60 per cent line plus experiencing basic deprivation. Since the size of the group which would be identified as poor by these alternative criteria was about the same, it was particularly useful to compare the types of household in each. In 1994, the 50 per cent income line would identify a rather larger percentage of the population as poor than the 60 per cent line plus basic deprivation criterion — 19 versus 15 per cent — but the comparison between the composition of two groups is still of interest. In Table 6.9 we compare the labour force composition of these two groups.

From this table we see that the importance of both farmers and self-employed among the poor is reduced when we impose the additional deprivation criterion and adjust the income line upwards, though this difference is rather less striking than it was in 1987. Households headed by someone in home duties, ill/disabled, unemployed, retired or an employee each constitute a higher proportion of those below the 60 per cent line and experiencing basic deprivation than of those simply below the 50 per cent line. The contrast between the two groups in terms of labour force composition is less marked than in 1987 because — with income from agriculture at a particularly low point — the number of farm households below the income lines was considerably greater in 1987.

TABLE 6.9: HOUSEHOLDS MEETING INCOME-POVERTY VERSUS COMBINED INCOME/DEPRIVATION CRITERIA BY LABOUR FORCE STATUS OF HEAD, 1994

Labour Force Status of Reference Person	Below 50% Income Line	Below 60% Income Line and Experiencing Basic Deprivation
	%	%
Employee	6.2	7.4
Self-Employed	6.7	2.2
Farmer	8.9	2.8
Unemployed	32.6	35.7
Ill/Disabled	9.5	10.1
Retired	10.5	13.0
Home Duties	25.5	28.6
Total	100	100

However, the application of the combined income plus deprivation criteria rather than income lines continues to make a very substantial difference to the actual households identified as "poor", as demonstrated in Table 6.10. This shows that in 1987, a common core of about 10 per cent of the sample were both below the 50 per cent income line and below the 60 per cent line plus experiencing basic deprivation — and so would be identified as "poor" by either of these approaches. Each method would in addition identify a further 6 per cent of the sample as poor, but the households involved differed between the two approaches. In 1994, once again a common core now of about 9 per cent of the sample would be identified as poor by either approach. The 50 per cent income criterion would now identify a further 10 per cent of the sample as poor whereas the 60 per cent line plus basic deprivation criteria would add only 6 per cent, and the households involved would differ between the two methods. It will clearly be important to elucidate in future research just where the alternative approaches makes most difference, in terms of the range of characteristics of interest.

TABLE 6.10: HOUSEHOLDS BELOW THE 50% INCOME LINE VERSUS
BELOW THE 60% INCOME LINE AND EXPERIENCING BASIC
DEPRIVATION, 1987 AND 1994

1987	% of Households	60% Income Line Plus Basic Deprivation		
		Poor	Non-poor	All
50% Income Line	Poor	9.8	6.5	16.3
	Non-poor	6.2	77.5	83.7
	All	16.0	84.0	100
1994	% of Households	60% Income Line Plus Basic Deprivation		
		Poor	Non-poor	All
50% Income Line	Poor	8.9	9.9	18.8
	Non-poor	6.0	75.2	81.2
	All	14.9	85.1	100.0

6.4 CONCLUSION

The definition of poverty in common use in developed countries is
that it constitutes exclusion from the life of society arising from a
lack of resources. Being "excluded" in this context is generally
taken to mean experiencing various forms of what the society in
question regards as serious deprivation, and we have in previous
research based on the 1987 survey used direct measures of deprivation to assess the reliability of the common practice of using low
income alone as a "marker" for exclusion. That research concluded
that a great deal could be learned by focusing on households
which are both on low income and experiencing what we have
termed basic deprivation. In this chapter we have applied the
approach to doing so, developed in our earlier work, to the 1994
sample.

Once again three sets or dimensions of items that cluster together, which we have called the basic, secondary, and housing
dimensions, were distinguished. Our confidence in the results is
enhanced by the fact that this structuring of the deprivation
indicators remains unchanged between 1987 and 1994 and at
both points in time the dimensions involved display acceptable
levels of reliability. The evidence we have presented shows that
between 1987 and 1994 there have been reductions in the levels of
deprivation for each of these dimensions and for an overall summary deprivation index. Focusing on basic deprivation, the consis-

tent result which emerges across relative income lines is that there has been a small reduction in the percentage of households below these lines and experiencing basic deprivation between 1987 and 1994. For example, in 1987 16 per cent of households were below the 60 per cent income line and experiencing enforced absence of at least one basic item, while in 1994 the figure was 15 per cent. Distinguishing households as poor using both income and basic deprivation once again produces a poverty profile that differs significantly from simply applying income lines, with fewer households headed by a farmer or other self-employed among the poor and more headed by someone who is retired or in home duties. Households with an unemployed head continue to be the most substantial group among the poor when a combination of income and deprivation information is used.

Chapter 7

Conclusions

This study has used data from a new source, the 1994 Living in Ireland Survey, to analyse the extent of poverty in Ireland and the risk and incidence of poverty for different types of households. An extensive body of research on poverty and related issues has been produced using the household survey carried out in 1987 by the ESRI. The 1994 survey, the Irish element of a new European Community Household Panel, offers an invaluable opportunity to update the picture presented by that research and deepen our understanding of poverty and anti-poverty policy. This initial study, carried out as part of a programme of research being sponsored by the Department of Social Welfare and the Combat Poverty Agency, analyses the extent of poverty and the risk and incidence of poverty for different types of households, and how this has been changing over time.

In examining how poverty has changed between 1987 and 1994, the key methodological issue is how the standards applied to distinguish between the poor and the non-poor should be updated over time, in particular whether they should be adjusted to take only price changes into account or whether they should move in line with average incomes. In Chapter 2 we addressed this issue at the conceptual level, reviewing the variety of approaches which have been adopted to measuring poverty over time in academic studies and in current official practice in the UK, the USA, and the European Union. Against this background, the view taken in this study has been that over any significant period, poverty thresholds indexed only to prices will lose touch with everyday spending patterns and expectations. Over a relatively short period, however, the way real as well as relative incomes evolve will affect perceptions of income adequacy. While relying primarily on purely relative income lines, we therefore also look at the way numbers under thresholds held constant in real terms since 1987 have changed. As in our research with 1987 data, we also combine relative income lines with non-monetary deprivation indicators in order to hone in on those experiencing generalised deprivation due to lack of resources.

Since this is the first time the data from the 1994 Living in Ireland Survey has been used, a detailed description of the survey itself was provided in Chapter 3. This covered the way the survey was designed and carried out, the data gathered, the post-sampling processing of the data, the reweighting procedures to be adopted, and a first look at the validation of the representative-ness and reliability of the data. While further work remains to be done, the survey appears to represent satisfactorily some features of the population which are particularly important in the context of studying poverty, notably the age and sex distribution, numbers at work and unemployed, and numbers in receipt of the major social welfare schemes. (The fact that similar surveys have been carried out in other European Union countries as part of the European Community Household Panel means that a harmonised data source will soon be available for cross-country comparisons of poverty and social protection: however, the data for other countries were not available to us for the present study.)

A central aim of the study was to apply relative income poverty lines to the 1994 data on household incomes and see how the numbers below these lines have changed since 1987. Relative income lines represent a proportion of average income, and thus move up over time in line with that average. Between 1987 and 1994, average household income (adjusted to take differences in household size and composition into account) rose by about 50 per cent. With consumer prices rising by about 21 per cent over the same period, this represented a substantial increase in real terms. The poverty line set at half average household equivalent income in 1994 was about £63.00 per week for a single person. Alternative lines set at 40 per cent and 60 per cent of the average were about £50.00 and £75.00 respectively.

Compared with 1987, the proportion of persons below the 40 per cent relative line had fallen or was stable by 1994, but the proportion below the 50 per cent and even more so the 60 per cent line had increased. The percentage of persons below the highest 60 per cent line was 3-4 percentage points higher in 1994 than in 1987.

Alternative aggregate poverty measures which take into account the depth of poverty shortfalls as well as the proportion of persons falling below the income lines, on the other hand, showed a consistent fall in aggregate poverty between 1987 and 1994.

Indeed, these summary measures were found to be lower in 1994 than they had been back in 1973, when the head-count of persons below the income lines was significantly lower. The implication is that the depth of income shortfalls for those below the income lines had fallen over time, and particularly since 1987. The overall trend in relative income poverty comparing 1987 and 1994 is thus that, with half or 60 per cent of average income as benchmark, the numbers affected were higher in 1994 but the depth of their income poverty was considerably lower on average. The conclusion one reaches as to whether relative income poverty had risen or fallen over that period thus depends crucially on the weights one chooses to attach to these different elements.

As well as purely relative lines, the numbers under income thresholds held constant in real terms since 1987 were also examined. The growth in average real incomes which took place over the period was seen to have benefited those on low incomes, with a substantial decline in the numbers below "absolute" thresholds held constant from 1987. For example, about 20 per cent of persons were below half average income in 1987; by 1994 only about 8 per cent were below that line uprated by the increase in prices over the period.

Using the relative income lines, poverty risk and incidence by household composition and by labour force status of the household head were analysed and compared with 1987. With the 50 per cent income line, about one-third of poor households were headed by an unemployed person, with the second-largest group being those headed by someone in home duties. Children face a higher risk of being below the income lines than adults, and households with four or more children are at particularly high risk. Comparison with 1987 shows a good deal of continuity, as would be expected, but also some important differences. The most striking changes were an increase in the risk of falling below half average income facing single-adult households, the elderly, and households headed by someone in home duties — with a good deal of overlap between these groups — and a sharp decline in the risk for farm households.

The falling risk for farm households is directly attributable to the unusually bad year covered by the 1987 survey, with farm incomes increasing rapidly since then. This will also have had a particularly pronounced impact on the summary poverty measures taking the extent to which people fall below the income lines into account, since these will be significantly affected by the numbers reporting zero or very low incomes. The evolution of social welfare rates for different categories of recipient *vis-à-vis* mean income for all households appears to have played a crucial role in the other elements of the pattern of results.

Support rates for the elderly and widows rose by a good deal less than mean incomes between 1987 and 1994, and as a result those relying entirely on means-tested old age or widow's pensions were on incomes at or about the 50 per cent benchmark by 1994, whereas in 1987 they had been above that level. At the same time, as recommended by the Commission on Social Welfare, priority was given to what had been the lowest social welfare rates in 1987 — UA and SWA — and these were increased substantially more rapidly than mean incomes. However, the scale of increase sufficed to bring them much closer to, but not quite up to, the 50 per cent relative income line. A major plank of social welfare strategy over the period thus will have had limited impact on reducing the numbers on UA or SWA falling below half average income, while the associated relative decline in the support provided to other groups will have increased the vulnerability of those groups. This helps to explain the fact that poverty measures taking the extent to which people fall below the 50 and 60 per cent income lines were stable or fell while the headcount of numbers below those lines rose. This brings out the importance of using those more complex summary measures as complements to simply "counting the poor".

The substantial rise in social welfare support rates in real terms, as well as the rapid rise in farm incomes and the fall in the level of unemployment between 1987 and 1994, are the major factors explaining the sharp fall in numbers below income lines uprated for price increases only.

They also explain why the numbers found to be below relative income poverty lines and experiencing basic deprivation also declined marginally. This finding was based on the use of non-monetary indicators of deprivation, developed in our previous research with the 1987 survey, to identify those experiencing generalised deprivation or exclusion due to lack of resources. The deprivation indicators on which information was obtained in the 1994 survey are mostly the same as those included in the 1987 survey. Compared with the corresponding results from the 1987 survey, the proportion of households in the sample doing without the items had generally fallen. The way in which the various deprivation indicators relate to one another was analysed, showing that they cluster into different dimensions in a manner very similar to that identified by factor analysis of the 1987 data. Three separate summary indices were constructed, for what we have termed in previous work the basic, housing and secondary dimensions, and the pattern of scores on these indices presented. The results show that between 1987 and 1994 there have been reductions in the levels of deprivation for each of these dimensions and for an overall summary deprivation index.

Focusing on basic deprivation, the consistent result which emerges across relative income lines is that there has been a small reduction in the percentage of households below these lines and experiencing basic deprivation between 1987 and 1994. For example, in 1987 16 per cent of households were below the 60 per cent income line and experiencing enforced absence of at least one basic item, while in 1994 the figure was 15 per cent .

Distinguishing households as poor using both income and basic deprivation once again produces a poverty profile that differs significantly from simply applying income lines, with fewer households headed by a farmer or other self-employed among the poor and more headed by someone who is retired or in home duties. The differences are less pronounced than in 1987 because the number of farmers below the income lines is considerably lower in 1994. Households with an unemployed head continue to be the most substantial group among the poor using a combination of income and deprivation information.

In conclusion, it is worth setting out some of the priorities for further research on poverty using the 1994 data, building on the base provided by this study. It will be valuable to explore a detailed analysis of the variation in poverty risk and incidence across a broader range of individual and household characteristics than are included here. The relationship between income and deprivation indicators will also be examined in greater depth, particularly in so far as they shed light on the risk of poverty across different household types and on the impact of changes between 1987 and 1994. The impact of changes in the tax and social welfare systems between 1987 and 1994 will be examined, to point up the impact of policy versus exogenous factors on the extent and composition of poverty in Ireland over that period. The fact that the same set of households have been reinterviewed in 1995 and 1996, as part of the European Community Household Panel, will open up new possibilities for exploring short-term income and poverty dynamics. Finally, since these Irish surveys form part of a harmonised EU-wide panel there will be enormous potential to learn from cross-country comparisons on poverty rates and incidence, the effectiveness of different policy regimes, and income and labour force dynamics. This body of research should be an important input into policy formation, in particular the on-going development and monitoring of the National Anti-Poverty Strategy.

Appendix 1

SAMPLE DESIGN

Supplementing the outline given in Chapter 3, this appendix presents a detailed description of the sampling procedure adopted in the 1994 Living in Ireland Survey. The objective of the sample design was to obtain a representative sample of private households in Ireland. The optimum sample design would have been achieved using a sampling frame which gave each household an equal probability of selection — an epsem sample. The principal advantage of such a sample is that it is essentially self-weighting. Under such circumstances ex-post reweighting of the data would be necessary only to address differential non-response among subgroups of the population when classified according to a set of characteristics which were strongly correlated with the primary research objective of the project. To implement this type of sample design one would need a complete and inclusive list of all private households in the country. Unfortunately, no such list is available in Ireland. In its absence, the best alternative is the Register of Electors. This lists all residents (aged 18 years and over) who are registered to vote in national, local and European elections.

Because the electoral register is a list of *electors* (persons) it can be successfully used to provide a self-weighting epsem sample of individuals. As noted in Section 3.5, the primary data collection unit used in this survey is the *household*. Although considerable effort was made to convert the Electoral Register from an *individual* to a *household-based* list it was not possible to do so because of differences in structure as between one region and another.[1] Consequently the target sample which was selected was

---

[1] The national register is actually compiled by over 30 separate Local Authorities, each of which has responsibility for maintaining its own register in its respective jurisdiction. In urban areas electors are listed according to address. Using "firstings" techniques it is possible to identify individual households in such areas. In some rural areas, however, electors are listed in strict alphabetical order (ignoring household order). This prevents identification of *households* and results in the effective base of the sample being the individual rather than the household.

effectively a sample of *persons*, not *households*. The sample was selected using the ESRI's RANSAM system. This was developed in the Institute and has been used for selecting random samples from the Electoral Register for over two decades. The first step taken by RANSAM is to reconstitute the basic spatial unit of the register (the Polling District or Polling "Book") into a listing of District Electoral Divisions (DEDs). There are over 3,400 DEDs in the country and these form the most disaggregated unit for which the Small Area Population Statistics are available. Once the register has been re-constituted in the form of DEDs one can then link the socio-demographic information contained in the Census of Population with the polling districts used in the electoral list. This allows one to pre-stratify the sampling frame according to any combination of census variables. In selecting the sample for the Living in Ireland Survey the following strata were used:

- *Province:* Four categories: Dublin; Rest of Leinster; Munster; Connacht/Ulster.

- *Urban/Rural:* Two categories: DEDs with more than 50 per cent of their population in towns with a population of 1,500 or more versus the rest.

- *Unemployment:* Two categories: DEDs with an unemployment rate of 16 per cent or more versus the rest.

Because none of the Dublin DEDs (Wards) was classified as "Rural" this resulted in 14 cells in the stratification design. After pre-stratification RANSAM forms a cumulative list of the population of DEDs (or parts thereof) until a pre-specified minimum cluster size is achieved. The first stage of the selection procedure involves selecting a sample of these Primary Sampling Units (PSU) which are formed by single DEDs or aggregates of several DEDs depending on the population size of DED and minimum population threshold chosen for the sample. At the second stage of the selection procedure a systematic sample of individuals is selected from within the PSUs. The names and addresses of the selected electors are then extracted from the register and prepared as quota sheets for the interviewers.

The target sample was selected as 259 clusters, each of 28 respondents, giving a total of 7,252. The aim was to interview all adults in the household of the electors included in the target sample. The version of the register used to select the 1994 round of the Living in Ireland Survey was the one which came into effect in April 1993, the most recently available at time of sample selection.

Some work has been undertaken on the design effects for samples based on the RANSAM system. Keogh and Whelan (1986) note that for most variables the design effects have tended to be in the range 1.5-2.0. The sample selected for the 1994 round of the Living in Ireland Survey is the first to pre-stratify PSUs on the basis of Small Area Population (Census) Statistics. This should have the effect of somewhat reducing the sampling errors. In addition, one aspect of the sample design is that larger households have a higher probability of selection than smaller ones. This means that the sample will over-represent larger households. This will further tend to reduce the sampling error in variables such as income where the variance is likely to be strongly correlated with the mean.

Some problems associated with the Electoral Register as a sampling frame should be noted. By definition, it contains only persons aged 18 years and over *who are registered* to vote; it contains some "deadwood" or blank elements in the population, resulting mostly from death or migration;[2] it may contain some duplication of elements (electors) resulting from persons who have recently moved address, who continue to be registered at their old address and who are also registered at their new address. However, as Keogh and Whelan (1986) conclude, this bias against young people and recent movers is unlikely to be serious except where the variable of interest is powerfully affected by age or recency of moving. They also show that the register is a relatively complete listing of the usually resident population and concurs well with Census data on total population numbers within each district.

---

[2] Although the presence of blanks in the sampling frame will increase field costs they will not introduce bias into the sample or adversely affect selection probabilities.

Appendix 2

REWEIGHTING THE DATA

In Chapter 3 we noted that in order to ensure the representativeness of survey data it is necessary to adjust the composition of the effective sample in such a way as to eliminate any identifiable bias which may have arisen from sample design or from differential non-response among various subgroups in the target sample. This is achieved by reweighting the data so as to ensure that the structure of the sample corresponds with the known structure of the population as derived from external, independent sources. In the case of the 1994 Living in Ireland Survey, bias from sample design could arise from use of the Electoral Register as the sampling frame. As noted in Chapter 3, the register is not a perfect population list. In particular, the register provides a *household-based* sample which is biased in favour of larger households and biased against younger, newly formed households in which the members have not yet registered on the Electoral Register at their new address. We discussed in Appendix 1 that the register can be used to draw on epsem (equal probability) sample of *individuals* and that this is what was done in selecting the sample for the Living In Ireland Survey. We then proceeded to interview the *household* of each individual in the target sample. As large households have a higher probability of selection reweighting procedures must directly address this important source of sample design bias.

In terms of response bias one finds, in general, that households in rural areas have a higher propensity to participate in sample surveys than do those in urban areas, especially in Dublin.[1] In the 1994 round of the Living in Ireland Survey we found a crude[2] re-

---

[1] This reflects a greater reluctance among urban households to co-operate in surveys as well as greater difficulties in contacting urban than rural households. There is a greater chance of someone being at home on at least one of the four call-backs to a rural household than there is in an urban household, especially a young urban household.

[2] By *crude* we refer to the rates before adjusting for deadwood or other ineligible elements in the population list.

sponse rate of 64 per cent in rural areas; 56 per cent in urban areas outside Dublin and 46 per cent in Dublin. Because of these substantial variations in regional response rates it is important to have an explicit regional dimension in the reweighting scheme. The final reweighting scheme adopted had three distinct steps as follows:

Step 1: Adjustment for Farm Households

Experience in previous ESRI surveys (as well as that of Teagasc) has shown that among farm households the response rate for small farmers is substantially lower than that of large farmers. This differential response according to farm size impacts on farm income estimates. Consequently, in the first step of reweighting we adjusted the sample structure of farming households in line with the population structure (measured in terms of utilised agricultural area). The population figures used at this stage of the reweighting were derived from the Census of Agriculture.

Step 2: Weights Adjusting the Distribution of Households

In this step we adjusted the distribution of households in the effective sample with reference to independent population estimates provided by the Central Statistics Office as detailed cross-tabulations from the 1993 Labour Force Survey. A five-way weighting matrix was used, based on the following variables:

1. Number of Adults in the Household (five categories) X

2. Number of Persons at Work in the Household (three categories) X

3. Socio-economic Group of Household Reference Person (five categories) X

4. Age Composition of the Household (two categories) X

5. Locational/Regional Variable (three categories).

This gave an initial total of 450 cells in the weighting matrix. After collapsing cells to account for redundancy in the effective sample distribution we were left with 224 cells in the weighting matrix.[3] Ratio weighting was used for each cell.

The Step 1 adjustment for farm size was incorporated into the socio-demographic ratio weighting at Step 2. At the end of this stage in the weighting procedure we had a weight[4] which grossed to the population total of 1,110,000 households as per the 1993 Labour Force Survey. It is worth noting that the most important dimension in the ratio weighting matrix used at Step 2 is the number of adults in the household as this addressed the issue of differential household selection probabilities which resulted from sample design effects.

Step 3: Weights Correcting for the Distribution of Persons

The third step in the weighting procedure involved using the weight derived in the first two steps to adjust for the distribution of *persons*. To do this we assigned the *household*-level weight of Steps 1 and 2 to each *individual* in the sample.[5] We were then able to derive a weighted sample distribution of *persons* according to sex (2 categories) age (11 cohorts), marital status (four categories — single, married, separated and widowed). The same distribution of *persons* was extracted from the 1993 Labour Force Survey. Ratio weights were then derived on the basis of the population and weighted sample distributions so as to bring the latter into line with the former. This meant that each *individual* (respondent) now had a weight which was based on the *household* level weight derived in Steps 1 and 2 above but which was adjusted in line with the three-way distribution of the population of *persons* according to sex, age and marital status. Each of these adjusted *individual*-level weights (call them $ILW_{1,1}$, $ILW_{1,2}$, ...$ILW_{1,13}$)[6] was then brought up to the *household*-level file. A new *household*-level weight was derived as the simple average of each

---

[3] The collapsing of cells took place along the dimensions of the matrix where it would be most expected such as, for example, in large (4 and 5 adult) households in which there was no person at work.

[4] Although in a technical sense weight and grossing factor are different concepts the terms will be used interchangeably throughout this section.

[5] At this stage in the procedure we included the 506 unit non-respondents (see Section 3.6) in making the adjustment for the distribution of persons.

[6] There was a potential total of 13 eligible respondents in each household as the household register made provision for up to 13 members. In reality, of course, the actual number was far below this.

such *individual*-level weight in the household. When this new weight was applied to the household file we found that it resulted in some marginal changes in the population total of 1.11 million households. A small scaling adjustment was carried out to bring the population total back to 1.11 million households, which left a new *household*-level grossing factor (call it HLW_1).

We then repeated the Step 3 procedure two further times. In other words, we assigned the appropriate *household*-level weight (HLW_1) back to each *individual*-level record. We weighted this *individual*-level file by HLW_1 and compared the 3-way sample and population distributions of *individuals* according to sex, age and marital status. We derived an *individual*-level weight (using ratio procedures) to adjust the sample distribution at this second iteration through the individual file to conform with the population totals derived from the Labour Force Survey. A second stage *individual*-level weight was derived in this way for each eligible member of each household (call these weights $ILW_{2,1}$, $ILW_{2,2}$, ...$ILW_{2,13}$). These new weights were then brought up to the *household*-level file, the average taken and marginally rescaled to give a total of 1.11 million households. This resulted in a second-stage *household*-level weight (call it HLW_2) which was derived from the second iteration through the *individual*-level file.

The above procedure was then repeated for a third time, assigning the appropriate HLW_2 to each *individual* record; deriving a ratio weight on the basis of sample and population distributions of persons by sex, age and marital status ($ILW_{3,1}$, $ILW_{3,2}$..... $ILW_{3,13}$); bringing these *individual*-level weights to the household and taking a simple average to give a final *household*-level weight (call it HLW_3). This was then marginally re-scaled to give a total of 1.11 million households.

The Step 3 adjustment according to the distribution of *individuals* classified by sex, age and marital status is important in view of the sample design. We noted above that use of the Electoral Register as a sampling frame may have introduced some bias against younger persons as well as among those who have recently moved address and have not yet been recorded on the register at their new address. This means that recently generated households, especially among those set up by young, single persons may have been under-represented in the effective sample. It is not possible to measure whether or not this is so because population figures are not available on households classified by their date of generation. Nonetheless, from experience with the

Electoral Register as a sampling frame we realise that some bias against young, single households may have entered the sample due to the design procedures used. Although the three-stage iterative adjustment to account for the distribution of individuals had a relatively limited effect on the household-level weight derived at Steps 1 and 2, it does allow us to address any potential bias arising from the relevant design effects.

The degree of change in the weights at each stage of the procedure can be gauged from Tables A2.1 and A2.2 below. Table A2.1 presents some descriptive statistics on each of the weights at various stages. "Step 1 Weight" refers to the adjustment for farm households while the "Step 2 weight" is the weight correcting the sample distribution of households according to the 5-way weighting matrix discussed above. The final three weights in the table HLW_1, HLW_2 and HLW_3 are those derived as the output of each stage in the iterative process through the *individual*-level file. HLW_3 is the final grossing factor used for *household*-level analysis. HLW_1 and HLW_2 are the *household*-level weights which were output after the first and second iteration respectively through the *individual*-level file. Table A2.1 shows that there is only minimal change in the descriptive statistics presented on the weights derived at each stage of the reweighting procedure.

TABLE A2.1: DESCRIPTIVE STATISTICS ON HOUSEHOLD GROSSING FACTORS USED IN THE 1994 LIVING IN IRELAND SURVEY

	Step 1 Weight	Step 2 Weight	Adjustment for Distribution of Individuals		
			HLW_1	HLW_2	HLW_3
	(Farm Households)	(5-Way Matrix)	(1st Iteration)	(2nd Iteration)	(3rd Iteration)
Mean	1	274.22	274.21	274.21	274.21
Variance	0.05	31,142.71	33,968.52	35,749.59	36,842.18
Skewness	4.79	2.59	2.82	2.96	3.03
Minimum	0.59	25.92	29.83	29.49	29.31
Maximum	2.49	1,887.79	2,005.92	2,033.47	2,067.04

Table A2.2 presents the correlation coefficients between the Step 2 grossing factor and the three Step 3 weights HLW_1, HLW_2 and HLW_3 (i.e., as they emerged from their respective iterations through the *individual*-level file). From Table A2.2 one can see that HLW_3 is very highly correlated with HLW_2 and HLW_1. The fact that the descriptive statistics are very similar for each of these three weights, as well as having very high correlation coefficients,[7] indicates that the extent of change in both the absolute and relative levels of HLW_1, HLW_2 and HLW_3 is not substantial. One can also see that there is a strong relationship (correlation coefficient of 0.90) between the grossing factor output by the initial 5-dimensional ratio weighting procedure as implemented in Step 2 and the final *household* weight output after the third iteration through the *individual* file (i.e., between the weights output by Steps 2 and 3).

TABLE A2.2: CORRELATION OF STEP 3 AND STEP 4 HOUSEHOLD GROSSING FACTORS IN THE 1994 LIVING IN IRELAND SURVEY

	Step 2 Weight	Step 3 Weights		
	(5-way Matrix)	HLW_1	HLW_2	HLW_3
(Step 2 Weight) 5-way matrix	1	0.95	0.91	0.9
(Step 3 Weight) HLW_1	—	—	0.99	0.99
(Step 3 Weight) HLW_2	—	—	—	1

(All significant at 99% or more).

---

[7] It would be possible to get high correlation coefficients if the level of *all* data values were substantially changed on a fairly uniform basis. Table A3.1 clearly suggests that this is not the case in this instance.

Appendix 3

ASSESSING THE RELIABILITY OF THE DEPRIVATION MEASURES

Confidence in the measures of deprivation provided by the various indices employed in Chapter 6 will be affected by our assessment of their reliability. Fundamentally, reliability concerns the extent to which a procedure yields the same results on repeated trials. The measurement of any phenomenon is always subject to a certain amount of chance error. However, while repeated measurement of the same phenomenon never duplicate each other precisely they do tend to be consistent from measurement to measurement. The tendency towards consistency found in repeated measurement is referred to as reliability. By far the most popular measure of reliability is Cronbach's coefficient alpha which can be expressed as follows:

$$\alpha = Nr \left[1 + \rho(N - 1) \right]$$

where N is equal to the number of items and r is equal to the mean inter-item correlation. In most situations a provides a conservative estimate of reliability.

Cronbach's alpha can be interpreted as the correlation between an index based on this particular set of items and all other possible indices containing the same number of items which could be constructed from a hypothetical universe of items that measure the characteristic of interest. In Table A3.1 we set out the reliability coefficients for 1987 and 1994 for the overall 24-item summary index and the basic, housing and secondary dimensions. (Here we included the heating item excluded in the earlier analysis.) The outcomes are strikingly similar at the two points in time. For the 24-item index the value for 1984 is 0.83 and for 1984 is 0.85. The respective figures for the basic index are 0.76 and 0.80, for the secondary index 0.74 and 0.71 and for housing 0.62 and 0.63. These results suggest that, particularly in relation to the overall and basic dimensions, our estimate of deprivation at both points in time would be very similar if any alternative set of indicators

from the potentially infinite set of indicators tapping basic deprivation had been chosen. In relation to the crucial basic deprivation index further evidence of the fact that the results do not depend on idiosyncratic factors associated with any particular item
is provided by the relationship between the specific items and the
overall index. The correlation between each of the eight items and
the overall score excluding that item fell in the range 0.38 to 0.54
in 1987 and 0.40 to 0.62 in 1994. Furthermore, exclusion of any
item would have little effect on the reliability of the scale. In 1987
for the set of possible seven point scales the alpha coefficients
range from 0.72 to 0.75 and for 1994 from 0.77 to 0.80. A similar
pattern of results is observed in relation to the other two indices.
The evidence thus suggests that neither the addition of comparable indicators nor the deletion of any one of our current indicators would substantially alter the conclusions we are likely to
reach regarding the determinants and consequences of the dimensions of deprivation reflected in our indices.

TABLE A3.1: RELIABILITY COEFFICIENTS FOR DEPRIVATION
INDICATORS FOR 1987 AND 1994

	1987	*1994*
24-item Index	0.83	0.85
Basic Deprivation	0.76	0.80
Housing Deprivation	0.62	0.63
Secondary Deprivation	0.74	0.71

REFERENCES

Abel-Smith, B. and Townsend, P. (1965): *The Poor and the Poorest*, London: Bell.

Anand, S. (1983): *Aspects of Poverty in Malaysia*, Oxford: Oxford University Press.

Atkinson, A.B. (1983): *The Economics Of Inequality*, 2nd. Edition, Oxford: Oxford University Press.

Atkinson, A.B. (1985): *How Should We Measure Poverty?*, ESRC Programme on Taxation, Incentives and the Distribution of Income, Discussion Paper No. 82.

Atkinson, A.B. (1987): "On the Measurement of Poverty", *Econometrica*, 55 (4), pp. 749-64.

Beveridge, Lord (1942): *Social Insurance and Allied Services*, Cmnd. 6404, London: HMSO.

Blackorby, C. and Donaldson, D. (1980): "Ethical Indices for the Measurement of Poverty", *Econometrica*, 48, pp. 1053-1060.

Bradbury, B. (1989): "Family Size, Equivalence Scales and Survey Evaluations of Income and Well-Being", *Journal of Social Policy*, 18(3), pp. 383-409.

Bradshaw, J. and Morgan, J. (1987): *Budgeting on Benefit*, Family Policy Studies Centre, Occasional Paper No. 5, York: University of York.

Buhman, B., Rainwater, L., Schmaus, G. and Smeeding, T. (1988): "Equivalence Scales, Well-being, Inequality and Poverty: Sensitivity Estimates Across Ten Countries Using the Luxembourg Income Study Database", *Review of Income and Wealth*, 33 (2), pp. 115-42.

Callan, T. (1994): "Poverty and Gender Inequality", in B. Nolan and T. Callan (eds.) (1994) *Poverty and Policy in Ireland,* Dublin: Gill and Macmillan.

Callan, T. and B. Nolan (1991): "Concepts of Poverty and the Poverty Line: A Critical Survey of Approaches to Measuring Poverty", *Journal of Economic Surveys*, vol. 5, no. 3, pp. 243-62.

Callan, T., B. Nolan and C.T. Whelan (1993): "Resources, Deprivation and the Measurement of Poverty", *Journal of Social Policy*, 22(2), pp. 141-172.

Callan, T., B. Nolan and C.T. Whelan (1994): "Income, Deprivation and Exclusion", in B. Nolan and T. Callan (eds.) (1994) *Poverty and Policy in Ireland,* Dublin: Gill and Macmillan.

Callan, T., B. Nolan and C.T. Whelan (1996): *A Review of the Commission on Social Welfare's Minimum Adequate Income*, Policy Research Series, Dublin: The Economic and Social Research Institute.

Callan, T., B. Nolan, B.J. Whelan and D.F. Hannan with S. Creighton (1989): *Poverty, Income and Welfare in Ireland*, General Research Series No. 146, Dublin: The Economic and Social Research Institute.

Cantillon, S. (1994): *Inequality Within the Home: Women and Poverty*, Masters Thesis submitted to the NUI, Dublin.

Cantillon, S. and B. Nolan (1996): *Are Married Women More Deprived than their Husbands?*, paper to Irish Economics Association Annual Conference, Dromoland, April, forthcoming, *Journal of Social Policy*.

Carney, C., E. FitzGerald, G. Kiely, and P. Quinn (1994): *The Cost of a Child*, Dublin: Combat Poverty Agency.

Citro, C. and R. Michael (eds.) (1995): *Measuring Poverty: A New Approach,* Washington D.C.: National Academy Press.

Clark, S., R. Hemming, and D. Ulph (1981): "On Indices for the Measurement of Poverty", *Economic Journal*, 91, pp. 515-526.

Coates, K. and R. Silburn (1970): *Poverty: The Forgotten Englishmen*, Harmondsworth: Penguin.

Commission on Social Welfare (1986): *Report*, pl. 3851, Dublin: Stationery Office.

Commission of the European Communities (1981): *Final Report from the Commission to the Council on the First Programme of*

Pilot Schemes and Studies to Combat Poverty, COM(81) 769, Brussels: Commission of the European Communities.

Danziger, S., R. Haveman, and R. Plotnick (1986): "Anti-Poverty Policy: Effects on the Poor and the Nonpoor", in S. Danziger and D. Weinberg (eds.) *Fighting Poverty: What Works and What Doesn't*, Cambridge, Mass.: Harvard University Press.

Davies, M. (1994): *Household Incomes and Living Standards*, Paper to the 23rd. General Conference of the International Association for Research in Income and Wealth, St. Andrew's, New Brunswick.

Department of Social Security (1988a): *Low Income Families 1985*, London: DSS.

Department of Social Security (1988b): *Low Income Statistics: Report of a Technical Review*, London: DSS.

Department of Social Security (1988c): *Households Below Average Income: A Statistical Analysis 1981-85*, London: HMSO.

Department of Social Security (1991): *Households Below Average Income: Stocktaking Report of a Working Group*, London: DSS.

Department of Social Security (1992): *Households Below Average Income: A Statistical Analysis 1979-1988/89*, London: HMSO.

Department of Social Security (1994): *Households Below Average Income: A Statistical Analysis 1979-1991/92,* London: HMSO.

Desai, M. and Shah, A. (1988): "An Econometric Approach to the Measurement of Poverty", *Oxford Economic Papers*, Vol. 40, No. 3.

Dubnoff, S. (1985): "How Much Income Is Enough: Measuring Public Judgements", *Public Opinion Quarterly*, 49, pp. 285-99.

Dubnoff, S., D. Vaughan, and C. Lancaster (1981): "Income Satisfaction Measures in Equivalence Scale Applications", *American Statistical Association Proceedings*, Washington.

Evans, J. (1991): *Measuring Low Incomes: The Experience of Statistics Canada,* paper to International Scientific Conference on Poverty Measurement, Warsaw.

Foster, J.E. (1984): "On Economic Poverty: A Survey of Aggregate Measures", *Advances in Econometrics*, 3, pp. 215-251.

Foster, J.E., J. Greer, and E. Thorbecke (1984): "A Class of Decomposable Poverty Measures", *Econometrica*, 52, pp. 761-766.

Foster, J.E. and A.F. Shorrocks (1988a): "Poverty Orderings" *Econometrica*, 56, pp. 73-77.

Foster, J.E. and A.F. Shorrocks (1988b): "Poverty Orderings and Welfare Dominance", *Social Choice and Welfare*, 5 (2/3).

Foster, J.E. and A.F. Shorrocks (1991): "Subgroup Consistent Poverty Indices", Econometrica, 59.

Goedhart, T., V. Halberstadt, A. Kapteyn, and B. Van Praag (1977):: "The Poverty Line: Concept and Measurement", *Journal of Human Resources*, vol. 12, pp. 503-520.

Goodman, A. and S. Webb (1994): *For Richer, For Poorer: The Changing Distribution of Income in the United Kingdom, 1961-1991*, Commentary No. 42, London: Institute for Fiscal Studies.

Hagenaars, A. (1986): *The Perception of Poverty*, Amsterdam: North-Holland.

Hagenaars, A., K. de Vos, and M.A. Zaidi (1994): Patterns of Poverty in Europe, paper to Seminar on the Measurement and Analysis of Social Exclusion, Commission of the European Communities/Department of Social Security, Bath: Centre for Research in European Social and Employment Policy.

Hagenaars, A. and B. Van Praag (1985): "A Synthesis of Poverty Line Definitions", *Review of Income and Wealth*, Series 31 No.2, pp. 139-154.

Hallerod, B. (1995): "The Truly Poor: Direct and Indirect Measurement of Consensual Poverty in Sweden", *European Journal of Social Policy*, 5 (2), pp. 111-129.

Institute of Social Studies Advisory Service (1990): *Poverty in Figures: Europe in the Early 1980s,* Luxembourg: Eurostat.

Johnson, P. and S. Webb (1989): "Counting People with Low Incomes; the Impact of Recent Changes in Official Statistics", *Fiscal Studies*, 10 (4), pp. 66-82.

Johnson, P. and S. Webb (1990): *Poverty in Official Statistics: Two Reports*, Commentary No. 24, London: Institute for Fiscal Studies.

Johnson, P. and S. Webb (1991): *UK Poverty Statistics: A Comparative Study*, Commentary No. 27, London: Institute for Fiscal Studies.

Kapteyn, A., S. van de Geer, and H. van de Stadt (1985): "The Impact of Changes in Income and Family Composition on Subjective Measures of Well-Being", in M. David and T. Smeeding (eds.), *Horizontal Equity, Uncertainty and Economic Well-Being*, Chicago: University of Chicago Press.

Kapteyn, A., P. Kooreman, and R. Willemsee (1988): "Some Methodological Issues in the Implementation of Subjective Poverty Definitions", *Journal of Human Resources*, 23 (2), pp. 222-242.

Keogh, G. and B.J. Whelan (1986): *A Statistical Analysis of the Irish Electoral Register and its Use for Population Estimation and Sample Surveys*, General Research Series Paper No. 130, Dublin: The Economic and Social Research Institute.

Lampman, R. (1971): *Ends and Means of Reducing Income Poverty*, New York: Basic Books.

Mack, J. and S. Lansley (1985): *Poor Britain*, London: Allen and Unwin.

Mayer, S. and C. Jencks (1988): "Poverty and the Distribution of Material Hardship", *Journal of Human Resources*, 24 (1), pp. 88-114.

McGregor, P.P.L. and V.K. Borooah (1992): "Is Low Income or Low Expenditure a Better Indicator of Whether or Not a Household is Poor: Some Results from the 1985 Family Expenditure Survey", *Journal of Social Policy*, 21 (1), pp. 53-70.

McClements, L.D. (1977): "Equivalence Scales for Children", *Journal of Public Economics*, 8, pp. 191-210

Muffels, R. (1993): "Deprivation Standards and Style of Living Indices", in J. Berghman and B. Cantillon (1993) *The European Face of Social Security*, Aldershot: Avebury.

Muffels, R. and M. Vrien (1991): *The Comparison of Definitions of Consumption Deprivation and Income Deprivation*, mimeo., Tilburg: Tilburg University.

Murphy, A. and B.M. Walsh (1995): *Labour Force Participation and Unemployment in Ireland: A Microeconometric Study*, paper to Irish Economic Association Annual Conference, Dromoland, April.

National Anti-Poverty Strategy (1995): *Poverty, Social Exclusion and Inequality in Ireland: An Overview Statement*, Discussion Paper, Dublin: Inter-Departmental Policy Committee on the National Anti-Poverty Strategy.

Nolan, B. (1989): "An Evaluation of the New Low Income Statistics", *Fiscal Studies*, 10 (4), pp. 53-66.

Nolan, B. (1991): Recent EC Commission Statistics on Trends in Poverty, Project on Income Distribution, Poverty and Usage of State Services Working Paper 22, Dublin: The Economic and Social Research Institute.

Nolan, B. and T. Callan (1989): "Measuring Trends in Poverty Over Time: Some Robust Results for Ireland 1980-1987", *Economic and Social Review*, 20 (4), pp. 309-328.

Nolan, B. and T. Callan (1990): "Cross-National Poverty Comparisons Using Relative Poverty Lines: An Application and Some Lessons", *Research on Economic Inequality,* 3, pp. 277-309.

Nolan, B. and T. Callan, (eds.) (1994): *Poverty and Policy in Ireland*, Dublin: Gill and Macmillan.

Nolan, B. and T. Callan (eds.) (1994): *Poverty and Policy in Ireland,* Dublin: Gill and Macmillan.

Nolan, B. and B. Farrell (1990): *Child Poverty in Ireland*, Dublin: Combat Poverty Agency.

Nolan, B. and C. T. Whelan (1996): *Resources, Deprivation and Poverty*, Oxford: Clarendon Press.

O'Higgins, M. and S.P. Jenkins (1990): "Poverty in the EC: Estimates for 1975, 1980 and 1985", in R. Teekens and B.M.S. Van Praag (eds.), *Analysing Poverty in the European Community*, Luxembourg: Eurostat.

Organisation for Economic Co-Operation and Development (1976): *Public Expenditure on Income Maintenance*, Paris: OECD.

Orshansky, M. (1965): "Counting the Poor: Another Look at the Poverty Profile", *Social Security Bulletin*, 28 (January), 3-29.

Orshansky, M. (1988): "Commentary: The Poverty Measure", *Social Security Bulletin*, 51 (October), pp. 22-24.

Piachaud, D. (1979): *The Cost of a Child*, Poverty Pamphlet 43, London: Child Poverty Action Group.

Piachaud, D. (1987): "Problems in the Definition and Measurement of Poverty", *Journal of Social Policy*, Vol. 16 (2), pp.147-164.

Rainwater. L. (1974): *What Money Buys: Inequality and the Social Meaning of Income*, New York: Basic Books.

Rainwater, L. (1990): *Poverty and Equivalence as Social Constructions*, Working Paper 55, Luxembourg Income Study, Luxembourg: CEPS.

Rein, M. (1969): "Problems in the Definition and Measurement of Poverty", in L. Ferman and J. Kornbluth (eds.) *Poverty in America*, Ann Arbor: University of Michigan.

Ringen, S. (1987): *The Possibility of Politics*, Oxford: Clarendon Press.

Ringen, S. (1988): "Direct and Indirect Measures of Poverty", *Journal of Social Policy*, 17, pp. 351-366.

Rottman, D. (1994a): "Allocating Money Within Households: Better Off Poorer?", in B. Nolan and T. Callan (eds.) *Poverty and Policy in Ireland*, Dublin: Gill and Macmillan.

Rottman, D.B. (1994b): *Income Distribution within Irish Households: Allocating Resources Within Irish Families*, Dublin: Combat Poverty Agency.

Rottman, D.B., D.F. Hannan and N. Hardiman, M. Wiley (1982): *The Distribution of Income in the Republic of Ireland: A Study in Social Class and Family-Cycle Inequalities*, General Research Series Paper 109, Dublin: The Economic and Social Research Institute.

Ruggles, P. (1990): *Drawing the Line: Alternative Poverty Measures and Their Implications for Public Policy*, Washington D.C.: Urban Institute Press.

Sawhill, I.V. (1988): "Poverty in the US: Why Is It So Persistent?", *Journal of Economic Literature*, XXVI, pp. 1037-1119.

Sen, A. (1976): "Poverty: An Ordinal Approach to Measurement", *Econometrica*, 44, pp. 219-31.

Sen, A. (1979): "Issues in the Measurement of Poverty", *Scandinavian Journal of Economics*, Vol. 81, pp. 285-307.

Sen, A. (1983): "Poor, Relatively Speaking", *Oxford Economic Papers*, 35 (2), pp. 153-169.

Sen. A. (1992): *Inequality Reexamined*, Oxford: Clarendon Press.

Sexton, J.J. and P. O'Connell (eds.) (1996); *The Irish Labour Market: Performance and Policy,* forthcoming, Brussels: Commission of the European Communities.

Smeeding, T., Rainwater, L. and O'Higgins, M. (1988): *Poverty, Inequality and the Distribution of Income in an International Context: Initial Research from the Luxembourg Income Study (LIS)*, London: Wheatsheaf.

Social Services Committee (1990): *Fourth Report: Low Income Statistics*, London: HMSO.

Thon, D. (1979): "On Measuring Poverty", *Review of Income and Wealth*, Vol. 25, pp. 429-40.

Tobin, J. (1969): "Raising the Incomes of the Poor", in K. Gordon (ed.) *Agenda for the Nation*, Washington, D.C.: Brookings Institution.

Townsend, P. (1979): *Poverty in the United Kingdom*, Harmondsworth: Penguin.

Townsend, P. and D. Gordon (1989): Memorandum submitted to Social Services Committee of the House of Commons, in *Minimum Income: Memoranda Laid before the Committee*, Session 1988-89, London: HMSO.

Van Praag, B., T. Goedhart, and A. Kapteyn (1980): "The Poverty Line: A Pilot Study in Europe", *Review of Economics and Statistics,* Vol. 62, pp. 461-465.

Van Praag, B., A. Hagenaars, and J. Van Weeren (1982): "Poverty in Europe", *Review of Income and Wealth*, Vol. 28, pp. 345-359.

Vaughan, R. (1987): "Welfare Approaches to the Measurement of Poverty", *Economic Journal*, Vol. 97, pp. 160-170.

Veit-Wilson, J. (1987): "Consensual Approaches to Poverty Lines and Social Security", *Journal of Social Policy*, Vol. 16, No. 2, pp. 183-211.

Veit-Wilson, J. (1989): Memorandum submitted to Social Services Committee of the House of Commons, in *Minimum Income: Memoranda Laid before the Committee*, Session 1988-89, London: HMSO.

Whelan, B.J. (1979): "RANSAM: A Random Sample Design for Ireland", *Economic and Social Review*, 10 (2), pp. 169-174.

Whelan, B.J. (1993): "Non-monetary indicators of poverty", in J. Berghman and B. Cantillon (1993) *The European Face of Social Security*, Aldershot: Avebury.

Whelan, C. T. (1992): "The Role of Income, Life-Style Deprivation and Financial Strain in Mediating the Impact of Unemployment on Psychological Distress: Evidence from the Republic of Ireland", *Journal of Occupational and Organisational Psychology*, Vol. 65, pp. 331-344.

Whelan, C.T and D.F. Hannan with S. Creighton, (1991): *Unemployment, Poverty and Psychological Distress*, General Research Series Paper 150, Dublin: The Economic and Social Research Institute.

Whiteford, P. (1985): *A Family's Needs: Equivalence Scales, Poverty and Social Security*, Research Paper No. 27, Canberra: Department of Social Security.

Williams, J. and B.J. Whelan (1994): *The Dynamics of Poverty in Ireland*, Dublin: Combat Poverty Agency.

Wolfson, M. and J. Evans (1989): *Statistics Canada's Low Income Cut-Offs: Methodological Concerns and Possibilities,* Research Paper Series, Ottawa: Statistics Canada.